MAIN STREET SURVIVAL GUIDE FOR SMALL BUSINESSES

Forward by
RON BALL

SAMUEL K. BURLUM

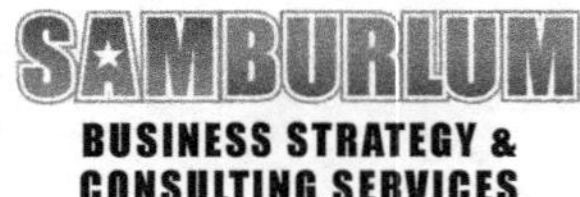

www.samburlum.com

Library of Congress Cataloging-in- Publication Date- Burlum, Sam

Sam Burlum's Main Street Survival Guide for Small Businesses

ISBN: 978-0-9988872-3-4 (softcover)

Cover Art: Novofex

Layout: Lloyd Arbour

Editor: Caryl Eissing

Consultant: Dan Hollis, The Magic of Selling, LLC

First Published 2018

Quantity discounts are available on bulk orders.

Contact samburlum@gmail.com for more information

DEDICATION

I dedicate this work to all the small business owners who have sacrificed their time; who have put at risk their financial well-being, security and future to follow their passion, and create value-based businesses.

I also want to dedicate this book to the career entrepreneur. It is the entrepreneur who transfers their value creation beyond the borders of Main Street and onto the national-international stage.

It is the small business owner and the entrepreneur who are the driving forces behind our modern economy. They are responsible for some of the greatest innovations brought to market and for the majority of local job creation. Without them, small town USA would not exist.

A portion of the proceeds from the sales of this book will be dedicated to educational and public awareness programs which share the message of the importance of supporting your local community family owned small business.

eye candy
Yes, we're
OPEN

TABLE OF CONTENTS:

DISCLAIMER

In a time of rapid change, it is difficult to ensure that all of the information given in this book is entirely accurate and up-to-date. This publication is designed to provide accurate and authoritative information about the subject matter. The author specifically disclaims any liability, loss or risk, personal or otherwise, which may incur as a consequence, directly or indirectly, of the use and application of any of the contents of this book.

The information contained herein is a collection of the result of research and personal experience, which may be cited from other sources, and should not be viewed as financial or legal advice. The opinions and personal experiences of this author may not be indicative of the results you may experience.

When investing money or taking a financial risk, make sure you have consulted with a properly licensed financial advisor, legal counsel, and/or accountant. No information in this book should be taken to imply a guaranteed result.

eye candy
Yes, we're
OPEN

ACKNOWLEDGEMENTS

I want to first thank all who contributed to the content of this book; the information and perspectives provided were critical in conveying the bigger picture of the message about the importance of supporting your local Main Street family owned business.

I also want to thank my fellow colleagues, business owners, and entrepreneurs for your continued commitment to creating value. It is your dedication to making a positive impact within your community that fuels this remarkable endeavor. Your unshakable perseverance is, in part, responsible for the creation of millions of jobs, economic value, international trade, and additional opportunities for future and developing business owners.

I want to recognize the many non-profit trade organizations which continue to "sound their trumpets" in advocating for the small business owner. From the local Chamber of Commerce to national trade organizations, these groups are on the forefront of the battle to keep legislative matters balanced and beneficial between the large corporate giants and the small Main Street family-owned businesses. They are the collective voice which fights for the American Free Enterprise System and for the rights of every small business owner.

There are legions of small business owners and entrepreneurs who share their knowledge, and pass it down from one generation to the next, furthering the legacy of the American Dream. We honor those small business owners who have spent a life time in the trenches and have a desire to share their experiences and know-how with the next crop of up and coming small business leaders.

Thank you to all of my mentors who assisted in strengthening my business knowledge. Ron Ball, Lee Iacocca, Robert Schmidt, George Blood, JoAnn Blom, to name a few. I also want to thank my current business partners for their support and words of wisdom.

Lastly, I want to share with each small business owner, entrepreneur and future business leader this motto: "*May you never give up on yourself, God, or your dream. Never quit.*"

FOREWORD

Bravo Samuel K. Burlum! He has given all of us a book that works. His information hits you where you live and immediately raises your game.

So many business books are filled with fluff and dominated by theory. Samuel does everyone a favor by explaining how entrepreneurial success actually happens. Burlum "pulls back the curtain" and shows you how to build your successful business.

I have been privileged to work with several thousand high performance business owners and have observed their special skills. In my success seminars I have delivered these principles to over 8 million people in 24 countries. Samuel K. Burlum lives these principles.

Samuel K. Burlum is a rare combination of "why" and "how." Even better he is an honest man who has built his accomplishments with fairness and ethical commitment and this is something God blesses.

Read this book carefully. Be teachable. Learn lessons that Samuel K. Burlum mastered as he has brought his dreams to reality. He will not waste your time. You should see this book as an investment into your business and its future success.

And remember, that the best thing about this book is that it hands you the truth of what actually works. That is more valuable than any untested theory.

This is your opportunity. Seize it.

Ron Ball,

-World Renowned and Recognized Public Speaker to over millions of people

-Recognized Author of over 12 books including: "Choose Greatness," "Secrets from Millionaires I have Known," "Your Ultimate Breakthrough," "Fearless Living" and "The Complete Professional"

-Author of the Weekly, "Ball Points,"

-Host of the television series "Choose Greatness"

More about Ron Ball at

www.ChooseGreatness.com

FOREWORD

As a small business owner, a professional business consultant that derives from a "big five" background, and someone who personally knows the author of this book, I am honored to provide input to this detailed step-by-step roadmap and mirror of what it is like to own and operate a small business.

This book provides the opportunity to learn, reflect and rejuvenate how you run your business, as well as start a business with an in-depth look into real life experiences. It provides insight into strategy, process, technology and change that starts and drives business.

It is estimated that this country runs on small business and employs over 50% of the workforce. As small business owners, we are the backbone of the country. This book gives us the strength to stay another day in achieving our success.

Take a chapter or section each day. Pace yourself and absorb the insight. Step away from your busy day and gain a renewed sense of strength, not only in this book, but God and Country, realizing that a great foundation in doing the "right" thing is priceless in the end.

To be successful, we have to prepare to pivot with the ever-changing landscape of the economy, consumers and other business challenges. These influence the behaviors of our customers and/or clients.

We need to stay current with technology and its impact on our businesses. One under-studied area of small business is risk management as it pertains to technology and data security. "Sam Burlum's *Main Street Survival Guide for Small Businesses* provides a host of solutions for implementation that can help a business operate more efficiently and profitable.

"Innovation is key." This phrase is tossed around without thought by many. One definition is "The process of translating an idea or invention into a good or service that creates value or for which customers will pay."

In business, *innovation* often results when ideas are applied by the company to further satisfy needs and expectations of the customers. In laymen's terms: it is about thinking and acting differently to spark a strategic plan that will position your business to a higher level of success.

Sometimes it is technology that can spur your business to experience an innovative moment. Sometimes it is a process, strategy or a change that transforms your business from a job that you own into a flourishing, emerging enterprise. It could also be all of the above.

Samuel K. Burlum offers in twenty-two chapters, words of wisdom; theories that have been proven in practice; and a road map of areas of business competency that are fundamental to any small business application.

As a consultant to "big five" companies, I have seen large corporations neglect areas of business that are crucial in assuring long term business legacy. It is refreshing to see this author provide expressions and wisdom herein related to long term planning; as the small business owner begins their journey, they are assured of knowing where they can end up.

As a small business owner, I encourage you to study the information in this volume. Not only is it an education that will serve your business well, by adopting all of these practices, you may save your business thousands of dollars. As small business owners, let's join forces in doing what we do best; our business. Enjoy this book.

Beverly K. White

President, BKW Transformations Group Inc.

a WBE & MBE Company

-NY NJ MSDC "Supplier of the Year"

-Certified WBENC Women Business Owned Enterprise

More about Beverly White at

www.theBKWGroup.com

Yes, we're
OPEN
eye candy
857

FOREWORD

I am very honored to be able to write the foreword for this book. The business advice that follows comes from the vast amount of knowledge that my contemporary, and friend, Samuel K. Burlum has apprised over the years.

Samuel and I met many years ago when he strolled into our local Amish Furniture store. We seemed to hit it off immediately. As we stood at the counter, we discussed business ownership which my partner and I were fairly new at. We also discussed the local economy and our individual experiences in the business world, as well as in life. His advice and guidance has made a large impact on my business and personal life.

I originally came from a corporate background. I was only familiar with working for someone else. Arrive to work at 8am, do the work assigned to me, leave at 4pm, and then go about my own personal business without a care about the company until the next work day.

Having the stability of a regular paycheck, weeks of vacation time and truthfully, no worries, was quite different from venturing out on my own, with my boyfriend, to start a business. But this is what we did when the economy took a down turn in 2008.

Working for 20 years for a corporation, and then finding myself "let go" with a compensation package was not what I was expecting. It was scary. I was great at working for someone but was I smart enough, strong enough, and tenacious enough to start and run my own business?

I took the leap and found out. Being a business owner is not for the faint of heart.

The steps that this book brings you through, from your business idea to planning your legacy, will help you through the ups and downs, as well as the triumphs and tears.

Having Samuel close, to discuss ideas, talk strategy and even get a "you're doing great!" comment, has been a great value to me. We have grown our businesses together.

Of course, nothing goes as smoothly as you would hope, but having a person like Samuel, as a mentor, helps during the difficult times.

The Amish Furniture Store, which I loved having, lead me to my current profession. While running the store, I had discovered social media. Coming from a corporate background, I had experience with LinkedIn, but the social media world was much larger than that! The love affair started with Facebook. Connecting with friends and family was the start, but watching how other business owners used Facebook and the other social media platforms, was fascinating.

Creating a social media presence for the store became one of the tools I used to "drive traffic" into the store. Showcasing our products and services, as well as showing our commitment to outstanding customer service and support for our community and other small business owners, cemented our value within the community.

All was going great until… on a very early July 3rd morning. A young man ran his car through our store, destroying two rooms full of furniture as well as causing so much damage to the building that it was condemned as structurally unsound.

What do you do then? Do you give up? Do you suck it up and start over? Do you wait until the building is fixed to reopen, missing your busy season? Do you move? All these questions, all of the heartache, all of the paperwork!!!

It was a horrible situation, yes, but it happened in the best possible way. What do I mean?

If the accident happened during business hours, customers could have been killed and I could have been killed. The only things that were hurt or destroyed were just that, things.

The driver walked away too. Thank goodness. Long story short, we tried to change locations. Without doing some due diligence, we didn't pick the best location for the new store. It was like starting all over again and we did not have the financial backing to hold out to be "discovered" again.

I went back to working for a company. What I discovered, and you will too, is once you own your own business, you don't want to work for someone else ever again. It was time to go back out on my own. I then began Follow Me Social Media Consulting.

If this book was around when I started this business, it would have become my business bible.

Throughout my journey from selling products to now selling a service was a shift in thinking and doing. Speaking with other business owners as to the benefit of social media, as is explained in Chapter 17 of this book, was an adjustment.

Having a marketing budget for your business is very important, but it is usually the first thing cut from a business's budget when times get tough and money gets tight.

Heed the words about marketing within this book.

Building your brand, building that brand awareness, becoming very clear about who your target market is and how you need to market to them, is monumental.

Get out into the world, talk to people. Network, network, network.

You don't have to do it alone!

✓ Set business goals!

✓ Find a mentor or business coach. They will see the forest through the trees and keep you on course to achieve those goals.

✓ Most of all don't get discouraged. Most people will quit right before they make a break-through. Study this book, take notes and refer back to it often. It is a fantastic guide for entrepreneurs, start-ups and business owners alike.

Thanks to Samuel, a huge proponent and believer in social media, and all of the other wonderful business people in my life, I am enjoying the life of a small business owner.

✓ I am consistently growing my business, year after year, as well as getting involved in my community and local organizations.

One of the things within this book that resonates with me is a quote that Samuel references by Henry Ford: "A business absolutely devoted to service will have only one worry about profits. They will be embarrassingly large." ✓

I have seen Samuel live by these words within his companies and community, as well as with employees, fellow entrepreneurs, friends and family. It is my pleasure to know Samuel. I value his insights, business knowledge and friendship.

Patricia Singer

President, Follow Me Social Media

and,

-Board Member of the Mount Olive Area Chamber of Commerce, (NJ)

-Social media trainer for the Morris County Chamber of Commerce (NJ)

-Ambassador for the Northern New Jersey Region of BNI

-Social Media Committee Member for the non-profit Employment Horizons

-Social Media expert on NY's #1 News Talk Radio StationWOR710 and iHeartRadio for the program Change Your Attitude / Change Your Life

More about Patricia Singer at

www.BesttoFollowMe.com

INTRODUCTION

One of the most commonly asked questions by small business owners is, "How do I compete against the big box retailer?"

Some family owned businesses ask, "How can we survive when so many large, big box retailers are taking over our town?".

Or, for those who desire to start a new business for the first time, usually it's, "Where do I start?". Starting a new business from scratch can be very overwhelming.

The trend of the transfer of wealth from the locally owned small business to big box retailers had its run of Main Street for the last thirty to forty years; however, in most recent years, the trend is reversing.

Due to on-line retail giants like Amazon, and platforms like E-bay, large, big box retailers have been losing ground as society has gotten used to being able to make a purchase of goods without ever leaving their home or office while having it delivered to their door in less than twenty-four hours.

Big box retailers are showing the signs of fatigue, as they cut back on staff, close store locations, and even declare bankruptcy.

Now I never encourage someone to celebrate someone else's failure, so please don't take what I say next in the wrong way. However, there are new opportunities rising up as a result of the collapse of the big box store model.

Even though we live in a world of being able to have everything we desire at the push of a button, I find many consumers still thirst for the traditional relationship between customer and merchant.

Nowhere is that more prevalent than in "Small Town America", where the small business ties neighbors, families, and community together.

With the trends of big box retailers reversing, locally owned small business enterprise has been on the rise. So as a small business owner, how do you capture a piece of the rising tide?

If you are entertaining the idea of starting a new locally owned small business enterprise or you are an existing business owner that feels there are areas of your business that need improvement (but you have no idea where to begin), I wrote this book especially for you.

As a business consultant to many small to medium sized businesses, ranging from the fields of senior health care, to salon and spa services; from an emerging consumable water product, to local educational centers; it has been my discovery that there are several areas of business competency overlooked by most small business owners in the excitement of starting their venture.

These key areas of business competency are discussed in this book, "Sam Burlum's Main Street Survival Guide for Small Businesses". Within these pages, I outline a number of discussion points that can make or break a small business.

The US Economy relies on the success and/or failure of locally owned small businesses across the nation. In this book statistics will continue to demonstrate that small businesses are relevant and very important. I also address these issues:

a. Why Main Street still matters…

b. Why do you want to be in business for yourself?

c. What are the chances that your/my business will be a success?

d. How do I decide what kind of product or service I should be offering to sell?

e. How do I find the financing needed to start my own business?

f. What are the most cost effective marketing strategies that fit my business?

g. How will I know what systems are needed by my business in order to operate efficiently?

h. How do I get my business to become more sustainable and profitable?

These questions and more, are aimed at provoking a conversation, as well as providing tools for the small business owner and entrepreneur to gain advantages in growing their business, regardless of where they may be in their business cycle.

Let us take a moment to examine issues that exist in our own back yard and then from a 10,000-foot view above. Then let's compare them to other business situations which other small businesses may experience, even if they are located across the country. The likelihood is great that your business challenges and circumstances are similar to other businesses.

The information provided herein is from experience. As I authored this work, I reflected on each area addressed in every chapter. I thought of a business situation that either one of my clients, business partners, or I had to solve, and the processes in which we solved them.

You will learn about how to implement policies, practices, and procedures that will help you better manage your time, money, vendors, and employees.

You will also learn about cost-effective steps on how to market your business against the competition of large big box stores, and how to provoke the ideas on how to be creative in positioning your business as the local industry authority.

Finally, I hope this book will provide an additional business resource. Aside from a step-by-step manual on how to establish or re-establish your business, I also offer resources and additional direction to organizations that were created to be small business advocates.

When I was hired as a business consultant, I was given a glimpse inside every business I serviced. What fascinated me were the common areas of business neglected, perhaps because the business owner was overwhelmed.

I became increasingly interested in understanding how my influence as a business leader could either help, hurt, or bring value to Main Street. Thus, through this book, I sought to take the opportunity through my responsibility of leadership to a new level; to assist in solving some of these challenges so that more individuals (without the luxury of having the resources to hire a business consultant) can find help.

As I did further research, it became apparent that I had an obligation to share the information contained within this book to help others become educated in these matters, allowing for more small business owners and entrepreneurs to have a chance at success.

I challenge you to read through this book, while putting a few of these ideas into practice. Many of the practices discussed herein have been utilized by myself, my business partners, and clients who put them to work in successfully growing their businesses.

I want you to have a greater understanding on how you can grow your business, and survive on your local Main Street. Please take notice of the following chapters:

In Chapter Four, you will get the "low down" on all of the stats behind what makes Main Street Businesses so important to our economic engine.

Chapter Nine takes a view of available funding to start or expand your business, and names some of the potential options that may fit your businesses' needs.

Chapter Eleven examines how to determine the difference between a business cost and a business investment.

If you care to know how to get your business to operate like a well-oiled machine, Chapter Fourteen shares with you a number of systems and programs which can save you time, money and frustration in operating your business enterprise.

Chapter Sixteen offers a host of understandings of the importance of taking the time to research and develop your brand image, insuring that it properly communicates its message with clients, employees, and the community.

Chapter Twenty provides a perspective on how to find and connect with other like-minded individuals who will have your best interest at heart.

Chapter Twenty-Two completes the cycle. It gives options on how to position yourself and your business for exit, whether it be by way of selling your business, retiring from your business, or leaving it to the next generation of small business owners.

I invite you to read this entire work, so that you can fully understand all of the tools available in growing your business into an overwhelming success.

Henry Ford once said, "A business absolutely devoted to service will have only one worry about profits. They will be embarrassingly large".

However, to be successful in serving customers, you need to have as many tools in your arsenal to not only survive, but to succeed on Main Street.

May this work serve you as your latest survival guide to conquering Main Street, USA.

Wishing you much success,

Samuel K. Burlum

eye candy
857
Yes, we're
OPEN

Section 1:
Main Street Advocacy

eye candy
Yes, we're
OPEN

– CHAPTER 1 –

Why Main Street Matters

Source: For generations, small family-owned businesses on Main Street were the lifeblood of local economies in most of America. They provided local jobs, accounted for the majority of the ratable tax base, and were usually the first entities to contribute financial resources to causes within their communities.

In recent decades, we have seen the disappearance of healthy Main Streets across our nation. Gone by the wayside have been the family-owned enterprise, where someday, a son or daughter would take over the store, continuing the family tradition as the go-to local merchant. In their place, we have watched the explosion of the big box retailer, run by corporate executive teams who have no connection to the community. These corporations usually redistribute their gathered wealth via Wall Street, leaving Main Street to fend for itself.

Main Street matters more than ever before. There are still some holdouts in small towns across America where small businesses are keeping the American dream alive. They need your support.

These are the businesses which survived the crushing blows of big box store competition and/or they are specialty businesses that serve the residents of bedroom communities, which cannot be replaced due to the unique services they provide.

So here is why you need to support Main Street, why it matters…

The small business located on Main Street might be owned and operated by a member of your family, a friend, neighbor, or someone who resides within the community.

Chances are that the small business owned by a local resident relies on other local residents to patronize their establishment. There is the old saying that charity begins at home. Charity need not mean a hand out; however, in this case it does mean making small sacrifices that make all the difference in someone else's life.

Yes, you might pay a few extra bucks for that pair of jeans or that appliance, but you are contributing and investing into the success of someone you might know locally, who in turn understands the value of being a positive influence in the community in which they do business.

Small businesses provide an income to municipalities. Each local store front or small manufacturing facility pays taxes, a lot of taxes, without drawing on the essential services provided to homeowners. Since business properties are zoned commercial or income-producing, they are assessed at a much higher rate than homes.

With more ratable properties contributing to school taxes, school districts have more resources to provide a better education for the residents' children. When there is a successful Main Street, demand to be a resident of that community is usually higher, thus driving up property values.

Businesses must pay for their own garbage removal and they do not require additional law enforcement or firefighting services to support their existence.

Local municipalities look to offset home property-tax-revenue with ratable property-tax-revenue. This creates a balance so that essential services can be provided to the community without over-taxing every homeowner.

A thriving Main Street denotes a thriving community. An empty shelf never sells anything, and that can be applied to storefronts and property values. If you have ever driven through a small town which had multiple thriving businesses, chances are you were more tempted to stop, take a look around and spend a few bucks.

Success breeds success, and people usually want to live and work in an environment where examples of true professionalism and caring can be experienced. A thriving Main Street can provide that experience.

Small business owners are essential to good municipal leadership. They are the first to feel the impact of local ordinances and statutes that affect property zoning and uses, and have the best insight as to the potential threat or protection such ordinances offer.

They are always the first to question local authorities about a business' right to free enterprise. Business owners can be relied on to voice their opinion on local political issues, and are the most interested in preserving the community's culture. They are well-educated about past governance, and the historic mistakes made by poor leadership, and are most willing to contest cumbersome local statutes that create a burden on the community.

In many cases, they put their money where their mouth is by becoming a part of the local political landscape as committee or town council members. Their motivation often stems from an experience in which they feel the business community is being abused by elected officials who are not responsible for paying the price of burdensome policy.

The harmonious relationship, or lack thereof, between local government and small businesses will make or break a community.

Small businesses account for fifty percent of job creation in the United States. Small businesses have fewer than fifty employees, and often employ people they know that include friends, family, neighbors, or folks recommended to them by a close trusted party. Small businesses are usually the first to invest into the local workforce.

Small businesses may not always be in a position to provide the same perks as a major corporation. However, most small businesses will accommodate the schedule of a local employee for time off to care for a child at home, or school, or a local event.

Often the local small business owners also own homes locally, have children in the school system and may even coach a local sports team in town, so they understand the importance of life beyond business. Many also become iconic employers for generations of teens getting their first job.

Small business strive to be a positive influence in the community, and therefore usually are the first to donate resources to sponsor a local little league baseball teams, football teams and other sports events. Many small business owners understand the importance of giving back, so they may volunteer to help a local non-profit cause, and may donate money or goods to that cause.

Business owners may be spotted cleaning their storefront windows, sweeping their sidewalks and speaking with local patrons to ensure customer satisfaction. Small business owners usually accept the idea of self-responsibility and service to the community in which they call home. These business owners may be the volunteers that make up your local fire department or first aid squad, and will close their door to aid a situation when duty calls.

Main Street Entrepreneurs know the importance of reinvesting in their properties, and in the community. A local business' economic growth is only as successful as the residents and community around them. Small businesses on Main Street have been known to reinvest part of their money into the upkeep of their building, or will take lead on a local project that enhances the value of the community.

They make their money locally and usually will spend their money locally, thus keeping part of those earnings cycled within the community. They will patron other local businesses in the hopes of creating a network of local commercial clients in addition to local patrons.

Small businesses are a symbol of American Free Enterprise. They represent the local resident who was willing to put at risk their assets or wealth. They put forth all of their own efforts in creating an opportunity for themselves and others, on their own hard work and merits. Rarely do you find the local business capitalizing on property tax credits or grant incentives from government programs. They have to be creative, innovative, and rely on their reputation for offering the best product and/or service to their clientele.

Small businesses commit to the success of their own enterprises and assume the additional responsibility to see that Main Street succeeds. In many cases, they put people before profit.

In order to protect the American Free Enterprise system, we must support Main Street. If we desire to get a handle on out-of-control property taxes, we must encourage local entrepreneurs to invest in Main Street.

If we want more of a choice as to where to spend our consumer dollars besides big box stores, as a community we must adopt the culture of shopping locally. In turn we must extend the olive branch to the local entrepreneur and provide the pre-existing conditions necessary for a small business to realize opportunity and success. If we don't, it may be the end of Main Street as we know it, and Main Street will be as extinct as the dinosaur. Once it is gone, it may never be brought back to life.

eye candy
Yes, we're
OPEN

– CHAPTER 2 –

America's Most Endangered Species

Source: A trend has been sweeping across the American landscape - the disappearance of small, family owned, individually owned and operated "Main Street Businesses."

Small business is the economic driver of the economy, the known provider for the majority of local job, and the main consumer of wholesale goods. Here, we will take a look at major factors influencing this trend and some steps which we can adopt to assist in reversing it.

America faces a number of serious issues as it looks to turn around its economy, job growth and infrastructure, while simultaneously tackling a number of social and moral concerns. One of the country's most valuable assets to economic recovery, local and regional job growth, and the creation of new innovation is the family owned small business.

However, in today's hostile geo-political climate, it is getting far too difficult for a small business to survive. Why is this happening and who's to blame? It is we who decide with our consumer dollars the fate of the economic health of our local communities.

Ultimately we are to blame for this issue that now plagues our community. The responsibility falls on each of us to change our consumer habits and ideals in order to reverse this trend. We vote with our dollars on how our Main Streets will be shaped, and the view today is dismal.

Small businesses face a number of challenges right from inception, which makes one think twice about wanting to own their own business. The amount of local and state regulations that a small business must follow chews at the working capital and the amount of profit a business will be afforded, even before the business rings the cash register.

Instead of embracing small business as a worthy community asset, civil agencies with police powers have honed in their focus on penalizing businesses for the slightest infractions as a way to increase revenue for local and state government. This occurs where such agencies and governing bodies have lost tax revenue as populations have relocated for lower costs and greener pastures.

Our nation needs every small business it gets, yet some penalties in controlled industries could potentially be so severe that a business would never recover the loss, and would be forced to close its doors.

Fees incurred to register a business will take a huge bite out of any initial investment. Obtaining building permits for construction and the cost of numerous inspections (which often include high-salaried professionals) are needed to maneuver through the complicated rules of local and state planning and zoning laws. Oftentimes, these necessary evils are overlooked when creating a new business investment budget by folks planning to start a brick and mortar business location.

Overruns in legal fees can jump to tens of thousands of dollars if a business chooses to locate in a town that does not desire to foster a business community. Yearly inspections, updates to state statutes and local ordinances, and ever changing regulations force small businesses to retain legal counsel on a regular basis.

Employee-employer relations are one of the largest risks with liability for a small business. The local store owner must spend valuable time in training staff, usually training the new hire themselves. They must hire on a pay scale that will be advantageous to the business's economic health but within the allowance of that business's available cash flow.

Local businesses are limited to the initial talent they can hire based on the available dollars within that business dedicated to payroll. Small businesses also struggle to retain talent when long term staff looks to earn more money or desire more perks beyond the paycheck.

One of the costliest benefits for a small business to provide is health care. Most small businesses only hire part time employees because they cannot afford to offer additional benefits to full time staffers.

In the profession of business consulting, I have observed a number of clients who owned small businesses. They lost key employees to competitors because they could not afford to offer more financial compensation and/or benefits to their employees.

Small businesses also face an unfair disadvantage of limited buying power. Most small businesses are limited on the amount of cash they can dedicate to inventory. Those that are dependent on product - based cash flow, such as a local variety store or hardware store, only have so many dollars available to spend on purchasing inventory.

These businesses are limited in storage of said inventory. Small businesses are not purchasing large volumes of goods to resell relative to chain stores that may be able to purchase for a number of stores. The result is that they do not get the same volume breaks as a big box retailer. This factor will affect the overall retail prices for goods and services offered by the small business.

Small business owners face a very burdensome and complicated tax code which impacts the business's ability to expand and grow. Many of America's small family-owned Main Street businesses are either sole proprietorship, limited liability company (LLC) or an S-Corporation. All of these business structures are "pass-through companies", meaning that the profits and/or losses of the business, as well as all taxes due (including payroll and sales tax), are ultimately the responsibility of the business owner.

In the event the owner's business does well, the additional net profits are then reflected on the personal taxes of the business owner. In a household where the business owner's spouse also works and is financially successful, it automatically pushes both earners into a higher tax bracket. Thus, the business owner must pay more taxes. This might cut into the money the business owner may have set aside toward either hiring more help or expanding the business's product or service offerings.

Most small business owners do not have the resources to hire a team of professionals to help limit tax liabilities; nor do they have the buying power of a major corporation with which to negotiate such things as payroll taxes and/or property tax incentives.

Local family owned businesses individually do not have the lobbying power to influence local legislation. Many are required to pay for memberships to trade organizations and/or business advocacy groups that will fight on their behalf on issues that affect the business's ability to operate.

Most large corporations have consultants standing by which are employed to lobby full time for legislation that benefits the corporation's business model, while also placing additional restrictions or regulatory burdens on small business.

As consumers, we have not made it easier for a small business to thrive. Much of their survival and success are dependent on the relationships created within the local community it calls home. A small business will usually support local causes and events important to the local demographic-geographic area in hopes to maintain positive relationships with potential customers. Because small businesses don't have the buying power of a big box retailer, the prices for goods or services will be slightly higher than the larger chain retailer.

Understandably, consumers have put aside the importance of having a healthy relationship with the local store owner in order to save a few bucks on products or services needed. Getting the most for our money on groceries seems like a responsible act. Yet, as consumers, we fail to realize the long-term effect these decisions have on those seeking to earn an income in our own neighborhood.

We have come to expect the bigger, better deals for less, without thinking about the consequences our buying decisions may have when we choose not to purchase our needs locally. This frame of mind for the consumer will ultimately create an economic ripple that will reach back into their own homes.

In making a decision to purchase products "locally" I mean from an independently owned family owned and operated business. A big box retailer located minutes from your home is not considered buying local. When we purchase goods and services from a local family owned business, that business usually will keep its revenue within the community, instead of sending profits to some large corporate entity located elsewhere.

The local small business generally provides a balance of choice in products and brands for consumers. Regional product brands get their start by offering new innovation via the local merchant.

You will find in many locally owned grocery stores, local brands and products manufactured locally will be featured; brands and products you may not find at large chain retailers. By supporting locally owned businesses, we are also choosing to support local suppliers. The quality of the goods that a small business offers is frequently better than the quality of products found at chain discount stores.

Our choice to pay a few cents more for something at a local retailer makes all the difference in how we shape our local Main Street business community.

We have to make a vote with our wallets to support local businesses before they all disappear, leaving us with chain store retailers.

Many of these local businesses may be operated by a neighbor, friend, or family member. As Main Streets become a ghostly sight across America, know that your spending habits were the vote that decided if your local business would exist or become one of the extinct species that helped build the America we now live in.

– CHAPTER 3 –
Buy Local

Source: When considering consumer product and service choices, do you consider all of the indirect cost and direct cost when you don't buy locally?

The holiday season is that time of year in which many travel to the mall to purchase gifts for their family and friends. As many scour the internet and the newspaper for coupons and deals on merchandise, they begin to plot their plan of action, as if they were generals prepping their battle plan to conquer the world of retail.

The dawning of commercials and circulars enticing consumers with blockbuster early-bird door-buster deals and discounts rallies the troops to ready themselves to part with their hard earned cash. It has become a custom in the United States to stand in a line beginning at 4:30 in the morning, the very day after Thanksgiving, in being one of the first people in that zip code to buy that new trendy item, thus officially ushering in the holiday consumer season.

As soon as the market and financial economist wrap up their turkey dinner, they transform into worker elves in the night, reviewing and revising sales projections and financial modeling, twisting and torqueing the hype around record sales of this gadget and that retailer, hoping and wishing that their information is right, then quick to get their sound bites on news radio and television.

By the end of the day of what has become "Black Friday", all hope that one of the largest retail-consumer events was successful enough to shake the earth from its axis, providing for new records to break next year.

I find this to be very disturbing. Not because of the power of the American Free Enterprise system, which I adore and love, but disturbing in the sense that so many have fallen out of touch with the economic engine that fuels their local community.

Of all of the "Black Fridays" I have bared witness to, not once did I see in a local community, people lining up at Joe's Hardware Store, or Jane's Family Clothing Store, to support them in making many purchases that would keep the doors of their local merchant open and alive.

On the news you never see video clips of people camping the day before at the local Five and Dime establishment. What are viewed are droves of people stampeding the doors of a big box store.

Many would ask why this is so troublesome to me. I would ask them, "How much of that money that you spend on that trinket you just bought from the big box store actually stays in the local economy?"

In an era of tough economic and financial times, during which our great nation faces the "Fiscal Cliff," most people are not asking the right question: "What is it that one can do to help begin to reverse the negative trend?"

The one power "We the People" can exercise is our consumer rights. We exercise those rights in the way we spend our money and where we spend our money.

Knowing how many communities are also facing fiscal crises, we should be spending as much of our money locally as we can, thus contributing to the stabilization of local economies.

So listen up small businesses! If you're going to win over the consumer, you need to know what you're up against. As a consumer, it is also important to know how your contribution will make a difference.

Statistically speaking, 80% of the economic engine of our country depends on small business (fewer than 100 employees, family owned, locally driven) to be the delivery system of goods and services reaching consumers hands.

Most people choose the merchant they are going to support based on two decision making instincts: the feeling of who they can trust (positive relationship and experience) and by power of auto-suggestion (which is triggered by the bombardment of repetition and invasive advertising).

Small businesses need to have an approach that is more comforting and more personable in catering to a patron's needs. As a smaller retailer, your best weapon is the relationship with your clients and the community.

Some people will balk at the idea and make claims that mom-and-pop shops will not have the things we desire, and we are foolish to think that local family- owned retailer could be competitive with a larger institution. I tend to argue. I want you to consider some of the next talking points that may illustrate where you save money, time, and energy by shopping locally.

There are several benefits of purchasing from the local small business. The obvious is that most local merchants do not have long lines or waiting time due to the personal service they provide. They are local so chances are, you won't have a long drive, saving you both time (waiting in traffic) and gasoline.

I have done a small study in just purchasing a pair of jeans. From a local merchant the jeans were $40. I drove less than fifteen minutes to the establishment. I managed to purchase the jeans within another fifteen minutes (after making sure I was comfortable with my product selection). I received first class service during which the clerk was very attentive and sincerely thanked me for being a patron of their store.

During the time I spent in the store, I got to know the clerk, who was related to the owner of the store. I learned how the store began. I also got to see all the wonderful letters and certificates of appreciation they had posted throughout the store, displaying how they contributed to many local community causes. I knew that dollar was going to stay within the community, and keep a person employed who believed in the brand of the store.

I decided to perform a field study at the big box store. I commuted an hour to the mall. The same pair of jeans I had paid $40 for was on sale for $34.99. It was an hour commute and about 30 miles from my home. I spent another fifteen minutes to find parking, and walked another ten minutes before entering the store.

It was about fifteen minutes before a clerk noticed that I was struggling to find the jeans in my size. She did not assist me, other than making the comment, "they are somewhere in that area", and took off to go on break. After another ten minutes, I finally found the pair of jeans I was looking for and went to the service counter where I spent another fifteen minutes on line. When I reached the set of cashiers, they did not acknowledge that I was a customer.

I felt I was treated as an inconvenience, as they were more engaged on discussing getting off work early so they could go "party". I then spent another ten minutes walking back to my car to face a 30 mile commute back home.

After all was said and done, I got home and noticed a scratch in my car door from the shopping cart that another mall shopper let drift into my vehicle.

I had done the calculation of fuel cost and time, versus the savings. My trip to the local business was fifteen minutes, less than seven miles, which equated in fuel cost of $1.23, (my car gets around 20 miles to the gallon), and $40 for the jeans. My total spent was $41.23 and 45 minutes of my time for purchasing locally.

The trip to the mall cost me $5.25 in fuel, and $34.99 for the jeans, for a total of $40.24 and 3 hours fifteen minutes of my time. As a CEO of a company, my time is very valuable. I could have better allocated the 2 hours 30 minutes extra time into being more productive elsewhere.

If I was an attorney that had an hourly rate of $475 per hour, I would have lost $1092.50 by trying to save a meager $4.01 on a pair of jeans. However, I had to go to the mall because the jeans were "on sale".

You cannot get all of the things you need locally. I am realistic and I have done the math on the difference on high items (computers, plasma televisions, and major appliances). In many cases the local merchant does lose out because they don't have the bulk buying-power of the big box stores.

So this holiday season, consider purchasing from a family-owned small business establishment. Chances are, a portion of the proceeds you spend at their store will go to that local PBA Little League team, or to the local community food bank.

Your buying power just might be the consumer dollar that puts another one of your unemployed neighbors back to work. And think of all of the time you could gain and put to better use. In the process, you just might become friends with the local merchant, who might give you a discount for returning to their store.

eye candy
Yes, we're
OPEN

– CHAPTER 4 –

Small Business Survival Rates

Source: Before you decide to dive into owning a small business, or set forth in your next entrepreneurial adventure, it is important to know the tone and state of the Main Street small business environment. Sam Burlum investigates some critical data and statistics that may help you before you invest money and time into a venture.

Knowing the score and hazards of any industry segment is critical when making decisions on how much money, time, and sweat equity you are willing to put at risk, as well as the expected time table it may take for someone to recoup their original investment. When a potential small business owner or entrepreneur has a clear understanding of the time table of the return on investment of money, time, and effort (including the probability of all the assumed risk) some potential small business owners may reconsider their line of profession and go back to being part of the general workforce.

Some, after reviewing all the data, may consider the odds in their favor and jump right in. Either way it's important to know what potentially lies ahead.

Of all the small business founded, how many of them survive and become a successful anchor in their community?

That is a good question.

The data varies, depending on what type of business enterprise, the region where the enterprise is located, the amount of investment required for upstarting the business, as well as consumer and economic trends. The Small Business Administration through their Office of Advocacy compiled data which sampled new and established businesses across a spectrum of industries. The data demonstrated that the longer a small business is active, the higher chance it has to survive and become sustainable.

According to the study, two-thirds (2/3) of small businesses with employees will survive at least a two-year term, with about half reaching the five-year benchmark. One-third of all new businesses are expected to reach the ten-year benchmark.

The Small Business Administration was quick to point out that, even with negative economic trends, these economic trends have very little effect on small businesses considered to be staples and anchors of the community. For instance, people always get their hair cut, people need to eat, and they need a financial institution to conduct their business.

The businesses of a barber shop or beauty salon, grocery store, and bank are necessary to a community, whether the economy is good or bad. These types of businesses have their steady phases of growth as mainstay businesses for consumers in a local area.

Usually the main reason for the rise and fall of a business is that local supply and demand are out of balance.

Hypothetically, let's say there are over 18 barber shops/ beauty salons in one town of 1000 people. If the industry within that local area was evenly split up between all the salons, each salon would have an average of 56 clients. If the average ticket of each client visit was $50, each salon would make $2800 per month.

This is not enough to cover rent of a store front in most places. The supply of salons and services outweigh the demand of the local market. Businesses not having a clear understanding of the local market and demand tend to input more supply than required. This aids in the failure of a business by default.

Conducting a thorough market research study will assist in informing you of the need for your potential business in a specific geographic area. It goes back to the theory of putting the right peg in the right hole.

Location does matter, and it is one of the key reasons why small businesses fail. The size of the potential customer audience and their consumer habits matter. When exploring the geographic location of a potential business location area, it's important to also consider the consumer audience's purchasing power and buying habits.

An exquisite, high end restaurant may not do well in a geographic area where the median household income is below $40,000 a year. Knowing these kinds of facts while reviewing this type of data is very important as you consider opening a business. It will increase your ability to make better choices of location and the kind of business you choose to establish.

It has been my experience that if a business can make it five years, it can make it to ten years. By the ten-year mark, you should be in a position where you could recoup some, if not most of your original investment and begin making a profit, depending on the type of business, and its product/ service offerings.

Most small businesses don't invent a product or churn out a market disrupting technology. Usually that is left to the career entrepreneur who is aware it could take decades before their invention or value creation becomes accepted in the market.

Even though most of the wealth in America is created and held by large corporations and their shareholders, small businesses are still a vital part of the economic engine today. According to the US Census Bureau, they calculate that out of 5.73 million employers, over 99.7% of the registered businesses in America employ fewer than 500 people. Their findings also show that over 89% of those businesses employ an average of fewer than 20 people.

The Small Business Association of America (SBA) also discovered that small businesses are responsible for the majority of new job creation. Smaller, locally-owned businesses accounted for over 63% of new jobs in the last decade. With the help of the internet, more small businesses found themselves engaging in international trade, where they could now source materials and goods from abroad. This allowed the small business to offer similar products as big box retailers at a much lower competitive price.

Some local retailers would, in turn, offer their products beyond their zip code. Sales beyond the local audience has helped many small businesses transform and stay current, as they take advantage of online platforms such as Amazon, EBay, and Keep America.

Some domestic products, branded as specialty brands or regional brands, are highly sought after, and make their way overseas because of the quality of the products. The small local retailer now becomes an exporter of these quality products to customers overseas.

The US Bureau of Statistics has found a drop in entrepreneurship. The rising cost of surrounding the process in commercializing an entrepreneurial idea, while investor groups are holding back financial investment until the product or innovation is almost market ready, have caused some would-be entrepreneurs to give up hope on their dreams. The Bureau supports this commentary; their study found that during a seven-year span, there was a drop of over 350,000 entrepreneurs in the US. These were folks once eager to take to market their idea, who became distant from their dream, and re-entered the job market.

350,000 people may not seem like a large number of people when you spread this number over seven years; however, the possibility that one of these individuals might have the next big thing shelved, possibly a vital delivery mechanism that would contribute to the next economic boom, is what is so alarming.

Not all small businesses can be seen from the roadside. Within the US Census Bureau, a study of small business owners revealed a comparison against the brick and mortar small business establishment versus businesses that cannot be seen.

Over 51% of small businesses operated from the home. Many of these businesses were service related. Many of these businesses were single owner-operated businesses. 23% of small businesses that operated from a home were also an employer of either 3 or less employees.

Almost 30% of small businesses are family owned and operated, where two or more of the household's members are an intricate part of the day to day business operations. Over half of all small business owners today in America, are college educated.

Examining the contributions small businesses have made to the current economy reveal that 99.7% of all employers in America are small businesses. Small businesses employ half of today's current workforce. Small business is responsible for over 60% of all new jobs created on an annual basis. Only 3% of small businesses are franchises. These statistics account for a total of over 150 million people employed by small businesses that contribute to payroll taxes.

Small businesses also account for almost 53% of all retail sales and almost 47% of all wholesale sales. The newest trend is that 97% of all US exporters of goods are small businesses, which is a sharp increase over the last twenty years, contrary to previously having large corporations responsible for the export of goods.

The latest question in the center of debate among economists is, "Which matters more: small business survival rates and statistics. or small business exit rates?"

Small business survival rates are the statistical data about the span in which a business continues and becomes successful from start up. But how many businesses have survived beyond the statistical analytics, and then were forced to close their doors? These businesses fall into the business exit category; this has not yet been vastly accounted for.

Business turnover rate data has not been readily available to explain these trends because the metrics on how to calculate these factors have not yet been completely established or accepted. As a business ages, new innovative businesses threaten its existence.

If you had a business that focused on repairing radios and television, and the technology of radio and televisions changed, it became more affordable to just replace the broken television with a newer model. People stopped seeking the television repair service.

This is a pure example of a business turnover not accounted for. Established small businesses that might have been in business for over 20 or 30 years, would now be forced to close their doors. It was no longer a service suitable for the times.

When an individual is considering what type of business to open, they must ask themselves, "Will people still need what my business has to offer in five, ten, twenty or even fifty years from now?" If not, you may want to rethink your business offerings.

A rule of thumb for any small business owner or entrepreneur in calculating their ideal concept of how much money, time, and sweat equity it will take for the owner to recoup their original return on investment is this: a) whatever amount of money you think you will need in the beginning for start-up and growth, times it by ten; b) whatever amount of time you think it will take for the business to become a success, times that by ten; and c) whatever amount of time you think you have to dedicate towards sweat equity, times that by ten. The reason is that the road to success is never a straight line; your business will experience growing pains. Its expected, so plan for it.

Once you have come to terms with the data, you can make a logical decision on the capital, time, and patience it will take to establish a successful business from scratch. When you are comfortable with the risk involved, a clearer self-awareness can help you decide on this journey you are considering. For some, they realize the risks are too great and they usually remain employed with someone else.

For others, as new small business owners, realize your role is important, as your small business matters contribute to the bigger picture. Becoming a value creator, you become a job creator and part of the economic engine that drives America. For those reasons, I wish for the successful survival of all small businesses.

eye candy
Yes, we're
OPEN

Section II:
Working on Your Business

eye candy
Yes, we're
OPEN

– CHAPTER 5 –

Knowing Your Why

Source: Why does anyone want to start their own business? Some individuals begin their own business as a path to make more money. Some people become an entrepreneur for the fame and glory that accompanies the company responsible for providing the next greatest thing. Then there are business owners who desire to make a difference in their community, and found owning a business as the mechanism for community wealth creation. We dig deep into assessing the why; why is it you want to own and operate your new business enterprise.

There are several reasons why someone wants to own and operate a business. Some people see it as a pathway to economic freedom, while others are tired of working for someone else and desire to be their own boss.

There are individuals who begin their own business because they want more time with their family. Some folks want bragging rights and glory, to say they are the captain of their own ship. Also, some people feel they need to prove something, and want to settle scores from yesteryear by way of being a successful business owner.

All the above are noble reasons for why one would want to start their own small business enterprise; however, it is not enough to keep you operating as a small business owner when things get rocky.

The truth is most small business owners will not see a profit or recoup their entire original investment for three to five years. If you are an entrepreneur with a market disrupting innovation, it may take you double that time to reach your break-even benchmark. Most people who are in business just for the money will lose faith and give up when they experience this lack of profitability for the first few years of their start-up business.

Someone in search of bragging rights, fame and glory will also be disappointed. There is very little in the way of attention for the local small business owner, who is looking to open the next corner store or new florist shop. There is no fanfare or marching band at your door. If you are privileged, you may have a local politician show up for your grand opening and ribbon cutting.

Just because you are now a business owner, you do not shoot into the stratosphere with celebrity status. If anything, you have become the enemy, the new kid on the block, that is the latest competing cash register now fighting for a piece of the local economy. You may become the target of local gossip and rumor, usually started by jealous competitors who feel a sense of entitlement because they were there first.

The "why," YOUR WHY, must be much deeper than for money or fame. Your why must have more purpose - full of passion and vision. Your why must have a soul just like you.

Your why will be what carries you through some of the toughest challenges your business will face. Your why will be the motivation of why you drive yourself to the limits on the hardest of days. Your why must be in line with serving a greater purpose; a reminder of why you should not give up on your dream of being a small business owner.

Some new business owners and entrepreneurs have built in characteristics as part of their personality defining how they respond to situations and also define "who they are". This is the reinforcement behind why they become business owners and leaders. Not everyone is born with these traits; however, a person can become trained and develop these traits over time. It will take discipline, time, and absolute devotion to the success of one's small business enterprise to refine these traits, becoming the key skill sets that a successful small business owner needs to possess.

A business owner, looking at the long-term big, picture, must have the character quality of unshakable perseverance. The sheer might of the tool and trait of determination is one of the key ingredients needed in the owner's tool box. The power to keep going, no matter how hard things may seem in the moment while having the attitude that nothing will stop you from reaching your goal, is critical for overcoming the hard times.

A business owner who has the tenacity to pick themselves up after being knocked down, not just once or twice, but multiple times, will separate the business owner and leader from the group of people who want to just own a job.

A small business owner must have an iron stomach to the cynics and critics. As a small business owner, your world changes. People you considered friends will not be quick to support you. There is an old saying, "If you want to find out who your friends are, start a business" The reality is most of the people around you will try to talk you out of starting a business. They might say things like, "you know nothing about being in business" or "that's a dumb idea, just get a regular job and be like everyone else".

They will not patron your business at first. Do not be offended. This is a normal human reaction. Your real potential customer list will begin where the list of your friends and family (you hope to support your new venture) ends.

If you are looking beyond Main Street, and are aiming your sights to launching a new product or service not yet available to the market, then you are in for a real treat. Everyone will begin to treat you like the plague. That is right;

you will become the one that no one wants to take to the prom.

The good news is that this is an opportunity to dedicate your alone time to your passion, your market disrupting innovation or product. Having the attitude that their opinion does not matter is important.

Most of the people that criticize you or speak poorly about your initiative will most likely be people who never bought nor will buy your product or service. You must show that nothing will stop you from obtaining your goal - to have a successful start-up business.

You must be a survivor, for in the moment of when it is the eleventh hour and your hair is on fire, you must believe you will get through this; that your business will persevere and deliver as promised.

You must be flexible to adjust your plan, but not your why. This type of self-leadership helps your business build a culture and reputation that people can count on, regardless of how challenging the circumstances. In this fashion, your business will become the underdog that many people will root for from the sidelines. This is where other neighbors, friends, and potential customers begin to believe in your why.

So how does a business owner begin to develop and test their belief in their own why?

There are a series of questions that a new small business owner can ask oneself if they believe in what they are doing.

It starts with the why. What do you want from this business? Is it money or is it a specific type of lifestyle that the profits of the business can provide? Or maybe it's the experiences and feelings that overcome one's self when they achieve a level of business success.

There are eight beliefs to consider while establishing the belief that you can be successful at your new business venture. These will help you reinforce your why.

<u>You must have a high belief in the industry you are now in</u>. Can it be done? Find concrete examples and successes within the industry that support your high belief. Score your belief at the beginning of your new business venture journey on a scale of 1 to 10. Go back and score your belief again after two years, then five years, and again, at ten years down the road, when your business is a growing success. To support your belief in the industry, review the facts of the product or products your industry has to offer. Are they affordable? Can it be profitable? Will people want it?

<u>You must ask yourself about your confidence in the industry's leadership, then take a reflective look at your own leadership from within.</u> Is the leadership talented, ethical, experienced, and effective? Score your belief at the beginning of your new business journey on a scale of 1 to 10. Then you can later revisit your belief months, years, or even decades later. Consider this: leaders take action, they show up, they are a product of the product; and they are consistent in their efforts. Leaders take risks and are willing to devote personal

investments of their own resources into what they believe, *the why.*

As a new business owner, you must have a belief that what your offering in either product or service serves as a great value. It helps to create an impact statement that begins with, "This product ______ (name of what you sell or the brand) is valuable because ______." Whether it solves a problem, or provides an emotional experience, your product or service impact statement must coincide with supporting your why. Score the product or service from 1 to 10. Then rate the product or service months, years, or even decades later to see if your belief had changed.

Does the math work? Money is math, and the math must work where, at a reasonable point, you will reach a break-even point, then crest over into profitability. It takes some due diligence, but each industry has a series of standard metrics which can measure whether or not your business is potentially viable. The data must make sense for you to believe in it. Score your belief in the potential financial outcomes, from 1 to 10; then later score these same beliefs months or years later.

What training tools are at your disposal? Do you believe in the information available to you that will help you develop skill sets in areas where you feel are not your strongest suits? Rate these tools from 1 to 10; then months and years later rate your belief in these tools again.

Do you have faith in the people you hire? Can they be trusted? Will they be devoted to the health and wellness of your business? Do they believe in the sense of purpose that the business serves? Rate your belief in their ability to help you grow the business. When your team is working together months or years later, rate the team again from a score of 1 to 10, and compare your belief to when you first hired your current staff.

Another belief you must be comfortable with is your belief in your support systems around you. At first your spouse, family and friends may not be crazy about the idea you now venturing off the reservation. However, at some point you must know where you and they stand. Rate your support system from 1 to 10; then rate your support system after things become extremely challenging, and then again when you begin to have some small victories for your business. What you will notice is that your support system, the people around you, may change alltogether.

Then you must rate yourself. Do you believe you can do it? Do you believe in your own why? Can you stomach the pain and the sacrifices that come with the territory of being a small business owner? Rate yourself today from 1 to 10. Then on a regular basis, rate yourself throughout your entrepreneurial journey, and you will find the one driver that helps you keep it all together will be your why. This over anything else, is where you must score the highest. You must have the utmost, ultimate conviction that you will be able to get the job done. All the other beliefs will rise and fall, and vary at times due to current business conditions and outcomes. The one constant is your own belief that no matter what, when you stare into the abyss, your why stares right back at you with a look of hunger and desire that your belief in your why is the driver behind you.

In the end of each financial transaction, the customer is purchasing your why. Sure, they could go down the street to buy their hardware from a big box outlet or clothing from the mall. It's because of your why that the consumer prefers to purchase from you. Your back story, your message, the culture you develop from within the business all become part of the why over time as your business grows. This is where it is critical in knowing your why.

Now ask yourself again, with a clean sheet of paper, "Why do I want to own a small business enterprise?" Ask yourself, "Why do I want to be an entrepreneur?" Write down every thought that comes to mind; then review your list. You will find within that list, a prolific desire (the why), that is your story, your product, and your brand that your potential client audience will be purchasing. Would you buy it? What value do you put on your why? Know your why.

eye candy
Yes, we're
OPEN
857

– CHAPTER 6 –

So You Want to Own Your Own Business

Source: So you have decided you are tired of working a nine-to-five day job and want to be your own boss. Maybe you are in a position to finally start that business you've always dreamed of? Possibly, like some folks, you have worked for the family business and now your parents or relatives are retiring and giving you have a chance to continue the family legacy.

Whatever the reason, you are ready to begin your new life as a business owner or entrepreneur. So where do you begin? What type of business do you choose to form? We take a look at the options available, and the advantages each type of business provides.

So you want to own your own business. Before you can determine the path in which your entrepreneurship career will be headed, you may want to take a moment to explore all of your options; review some of the hard facts about becoming an entrepreneur in today's economic and technology climate.

There are a number of types of businesses that you can choose from, spanning thousands of product and/or service categories and industries.

The most common business is a sole proprietorship. This type of business is more localized and is usually operated by the owner. Most sole proprietorships have one to a few employees, sometimes involving family members and relatives as the majority of the staff. In a sole proprietorship, one person is responsible for all of the decisions, operations, sales and marketing, and advertising.

The advantage of this kind of business is that the owner is in complete control of what kinds of products and/or services are offered, the hours of operation, who to hire/fire, and the success and/or failure of that said business. In some cases, a sole proprietorship is passed down from generation to generation.

Within a sole proprietorship, you will find a single operator; someone who has decided to specialize in one area or craft of expertise, and is for hire on a project-to-project basis. Commonly found examples of a sole proprietorship include a locally owned barber shop or hair salon, a cafe, deli, or restaurant, an automotive repair shop, a single doctor's practice, a certified public accountant practice, a single lawyer practice, or local hardware store.

The downside of having a sole proprietorship is that you are responsible for everything. Even if you do not have all of the acquired skill sets in every area of business, you must step up and handle each of these situations. They are part of the operations; no matter the type of product or service being offered.

For instance, if you are very good at marketing but not very skilled at bookkeeping, you are still responsible for having the knowledge to be able to do your own accounting. In situations where you might be very good at one area of your business, but lack the skill sets in other areas, you have a few options.

A sole proprietor can enroll in additional educational or training classes and seminars to enhance or acquire new skills. They can source out specific tasks to other professionals that specialize in areas of skill sets the sole proprietor recognizes they themselves do not have.

Some folks that choose to start their own business, but don't want to start from scratch, may choose to buy a franchise, in a specific area of product or service-offering. The upside of a franchise is that a sole proprietor usually gets corporate support, branding, marketing, and advertising support, as well as a working model on how the franchise must function. Franchises are, in essence, a ready-made business.

Most franchises require a substantial monetary investment up-front, requiring a sole proprietor to adhere to all of the terms and conditions of the franchise agreement.

Limitations of a franchise are that the owner-operator of the franchise location cannot change the corporate model. They have very little or no control over the cost of goods sold, pricing, advertising, store location design and appearance. When owning a franchise, the owner-operator has very limited or little way of adding in their own creative input or control into their local business, and cannot change the corporate model.

Advantages of a franchise are that most of the difficult guess work is eliminated from the equation as it relates to product development and product offerings, branding and marketing, advertising, product/service pricing, business model, and even employee hiring and training programs. Franchise models have the buying power of media buying and launching national advertising campaigns, aimed at driving potential customers to the door of local stores. Most franchises have major brand recognition; consumers immediately recognize the product and services offered.

An alternative to a franchise is a cooperative membership model. Co-operative membership business models are popular in the industry segments of grocery stores, pharmacies, hardware stores, auto part stores, and other regional variety stores.

Some of the most well recognized co-op brands include Hardware Hank, Ace Hardware, True Value, NAPA Auto Parts, and IGA. The co-operative business model consists of many independently owned stores by individual sole proprietors that pay a fee to use the headlined branding, and also agree to only buy all of their goods from the warehouse that supports that specific brand.

For instance, a Hardware Hank hardware store is independently owned; however, the co-op owner has an agreement to purchase the inventory it desires to sell exclusively from the warehouse that supports that brand. In the case of Hardware Hank, they must purchase their inventory from United Hardware.

A co-operative model allows for the independent sole proprietors to have more control over their own stores, with the support of name recognition of a national brand. Part of the fees and costs paid by the store owner to their co-operative provider assist in regional and/or national advertising campaigns, product development and introduction, and supports the central distribution center.

In a co-operative business model, the members each have a vote or can cast a suggestion in how to improve the overall co-operative central focus. In essence, every co-op member is an owner in the corporate side of the business. Store owners still have the freedom to market to their local community, while rules and regulations on how to operate their individual store are not as rigid as a franchise.

Maybe you and a friend or a family member both have something equally important to contribute to a business enterprise, and decide it would be advantageous to team up with this person to start a business. This type of business is a partnership.

More sophisticated types of partnerships are limited liability partnerships. A partnership can have one or more partners that have agreed to either contribute money, time, property, and/or labor, singularly or in a combination of any of these areas equally or in part.

One of the keys to a successful working partnership is to have a very strong operating agreement in place, signed by all of the partners, so that each person is aware of how the business should function; how decisions are made; how to resolve a dispute among partners; and, how to distribute profits/losses to the members of the business.

Each partnership is different. In some situations, each partner may have an ability to contribute a greater amount of resource than the other partner. Some partnerships have a model that one can mimic, such as the model used for vetting partners in a law firm or doctor's practice. As the saying also goes, be careful who you choose to partner with.

Two people that may have the same passion for the same type of business in the same industry may not always be the best fit. Differences in opinion on how money should be treated, how people should be paid, where a business focuses its growth on, what products and/or services are offered, and even a difference in core values can either keep a partnership working or split it apart.

Before you decide to enter a partnership, make sure that both parties have a clear understanding of the rules of engagement, expectations, and commitments.

Some businesses are employee-owned. An employee-owned business is one in which every employee has a stake in the business. This type of business model encourages ownership responsibility throughout every level of job duty, allowing for every employee to feel that their voice and contribution is recognized and heard.

The employee-owned company model was designed to elevate the "team" operating model, with hopes that no employee feels that if they choose to "slack off on the job", their lack of taking responsibility <u>only</u> hurts the company. Within the employee owned structure, every employee and manager are viewed as being on the same team, having equal footing, and managing is just one of the roles that allow for better continuity of the team's efforts.

On the flip side of an employee-owned business, if the business is too small, employees may feel they are entitled to more than the founders or stakeholders that have more financial risk on the table. Employee-owned businesses have become popular in the industry segments of grocery stores, variety stores, club stores, car rentals, and other specialty industries.

Employees have no upfront cost; their ownership stake is part of their compensation. Not every employee at an employee-owned company is an owner, for it takes time to achieve and earn this status. The better one performs, and the more responsibility an employee assumes, the more stake they can earn. This incentive allows for people in specific roles to take on additional work, knowing their contribution adds to the overall success of the business enterprise and they will receive a benefit of that.

A corporation is reserved for the career entrepreneur. A sole proprietorship becomes a corporation when the individual's idea is widely expanded from the local market and offered to a national or worldwide market. The sole proprietorship has outgrown its local market, and now employs a large number of employees, and has a deep infrastructure in place to support larger business enterprise orders. This type of company may also offer multiple products and services to the general consumer, wholesale market, other commercial and industrial businesses, and clients.

A corporation may have multiple investors who all have an ownership stake, known as shareholders. A corporation usually has a board of directors, with a company structure that includes executives, management, employees, vendors, suppliers, as well as outside third party professionals and consultants. When it comes to reporting requirements, a corporation has different legal protections and responsibilities than a sole proprietorship does. Tax treatment is also handled differently depending on the type of corporation structure.

There are two types of corporations: "S" corporations

and "C" corporations. The major differences between these two types of corporate structures are in the areas of ownership, shareholder rights, and taxation.

An "S" corporation can have no more than 100 shareholders, have only one type of share category, and in tax treatment are another form of a pass through. This means that profits and/or loss liabilities are passed to the owners/founders. "C" corporations have the ability to have different stock categories; voting rights can be segmented out differently, based on a series of financial contribution or management factors; profits/dividends have two tax treatments.

First, the corporation is taxed on gross revenue and profits; then each shareholder is taxed on the dividend they receive from the company as a result of their return on their risk.

A simpler version of a corporation is the Limited Liability Company (LLC). An LLC will allow for a sole proprietor or group of partners many of the same legal protections that can be found associated with a corporation.

However, the major differences are tax treatment and ownership structure. LLC's cannot sell shares, and protections afforded to a LLC can be revoked and the liability forwarded to the owner(s) if the business does not stay within compliance. It is always better to get an expert opinion from a professional before you decide on the direction of your business structure.

Many factors have to be considered before making a final decision, including the type of business, what products and services you plan to offer, the audience of consumer you plan to attract; how big or small you wish to grow your business, and how much of your finances you will be putting at risk.

The SBA offers many resources on their website, as does the United States Department of Commerce regarding how to start a business. You can also engage the services of a business consultant to conduct research on your behalf and provide you with options that best fit your entrepreneurial vision.

– CHAPTER 7 –

Product or Service

Source: Now that you have decided on the type of business you desire to own, a small business owner must carefully consider which products and/or services it will offer to potential customers. Do you want to have a retail business or be a service-based provider? There are advantages and disadvantages to both types of business offering situations.

Making the decision to become a business owner is a substantial undertaking. After the initial decision to do so, you will need to give consideration to the next steps which include your specific industry interest, and whether you desire to offer a product, a service, or both.

Owning a business that sells products can be a costly investment depending on the type of business you are planning on opening. On the other hand, selling services that are intangible relies on your ability to transfer confidence about your expert skill sets. In choosing whether to offer a product or to be a service oriented business, there are advantages and disadvantages with the types of value proposition offerings.

Developing a business that sells products can offer several advantages in terms of business growth and financial reward. Products are tangible items; they can be held in one's hand prior to any financial exchange. Products allow an individual to identify with a product quicker since they can use their senses to make a judgement and a decision to purchase the product. You can see what a product looks like, how it tastes (if is a food product), how it smells, how it sounds (if it makes sounds), and how it feels (like clothing or a tool that you hold in your hand).

Consumers have an opportunity to visually inspect the product they may choose to purchase, which allows consumers to decrease their risk when purchasing the product. Products are simpler to validate by the potential end user. The customer has an "out" if they are not happy with their purchase; usually they can return the item to the store.

A customer can predict what the expectation might be, based on previous purchases of the same or similar product. There is a sense of product continuity; each time a customer purchases a said product, they feel more comfortable based on their previous buying decision. This leads to a quicker closing rate on the sale of the product. If someone chooses not to purchase the product, then it can be reserved for the next potential customer.

Most national brand products already have large marketing machines in place to drive public awareness and educate potential customers about the product offered in your store. Having these products in your store, where there is already an existing market demand, increases the chances of potential foot traffic. The product business relies on brand recognition.

In today's market, products can be sold globally, and shipped just about anywhere. Store owners are no longer limited to just their own zip code. With product sales, advertising and marketing can be targeted toward a larger demographic and geographic set of potential clients. The name of the sales game for products is to sell product in either large volume to a small number of clients or take many small orders from a high volume of clients.

The downside of a product-based business is initial investment into a store location and the upfront cost of inventory. According to the International Council of Shopping Centers, the average cost per square foot of retail lease space in 2015 was $41 per square foot. Ace Hardware advocates that the optimum store size should be 10,000 square foot, which could be quite costly for many new business owners just beginning.

The investment needed to fully stock a new hardware store or family owned pharmacy capable of competing against a big box retailer location will cost up to millions of dollars in order to be ready to open their doors, and have ample supply of goods available for consumers. In today's market, consumers demand more product choices in multiple product categories, so stores must offer the customer service model of convenience. This allows the business owner to make available these multiple choices and product mix to potential customers in order to be dubbed the "one stop shop".

When your business is a product driven model, there are additional risks you must be aware of. Even if you have the proper funding to fill your store and/or warehouse full of inventory, there are still the issues of shrink and loss due to damages.

Shrink is internal theft from employees, which does happen. An employee may not think it's a big deal to remove a product for their own sample use, however, when that employee does not account for the product, it results in shrink. Some employees do intentionally steal products from their employers, as they feel one box or can will not hurt anyone, but it does when it adds up in the loss column.

Damaged inventory is also a loss to the store owner. Inventory that is either shipped or received damaged, is inventory lost. Most damages happen during the shipping process to and from the warehouse. Sometimes a forklift operator may not have noticed that they misjudged moving a pallet of product around, and it becomes dented and damaged.

Some disadvantages of having a product-based business can be overcome, allowing for higher profitability and customer satisfaction. Having an accurate inventory control system in place will allow for you to house just the right amount of inventory in your store, based on historical consumer data, thus limiting the risk of having overstocked an item. By offering a program to your clients by which they can order whatever they need, (not yet stocked in your store) with a two or three day turn around, will allow for you to service the sale, while not having to stock everything that may not sell on a regular basis.

Employee training on the importance of monitoring shrink, as well as reviewing the best practices in logistics, shipping, receiving, and warehousing, will assist you in decreasing lost or damaged inventory. There is no getting around the cost of renting space; however, there are some things you can do to get more for your rental dollar, such as negotiating for grounds keeping services, community fees, and other areas of financial value in your lease agreement.

Today, it's not just about what is on the shelf at your store front. There are several online tools available in marketing a product over the internet, allowing you to make contact with potential clients outside your physical store location's zip code. Amazon has become the premier platform of choice for selling merchandise online by local merchants, followed by EBAY, and other partnered sales sites such as Keep America.com, which promote products that are manufactured stateside.

With the evolution of online commerce and social media marketing, the traditional brick and mortar store front is only half of the available opportunity for many locally owned retailer merchants offering unique brands and/or specialty product.

Marketing a product-based business has more options for the business owner. A business owner can piggyback on national product recognition and ad campaigns in creating awareness that these popular products are at his or her store. If your store is part of a cooperative group, the cooperative group usually supplies a recipe for investing into local brand awareness, in contrast to other competing products and stores.

Marketing and advertising options are endless. You must ask yourself, what are you really selling? In many cases, products have a brand identity that must accompany the product.

The cost of setting up a product-based business varies depending on a number of variables. These costs will be driven partially by the decision you, the business owner, makes. Do you choose to sell a limited product line from home as an internet-based business or are you prepared to open up a full blown retail location, with thousands of product selections? Do you start small with a limited store front or do you take a chance and open a large retail location? How many employees do you think you will need in the beginning to staff your operation or do you start off as the single owner-operator?

Some new business owners opt to offer their expertise, as well as their skill sets, in the form of services offered. The upside to owning a business that is more service-oriented is that you have minimal, if any, inventory to stock.

Your services offered are not limited to the product's limitations. For example, if your service business is building decks, you can design and build a deck according to the vision the potential client may have. A service business allows for the business owner to be more personalized and creative when providing services to each individual client.

Your service should focus on solving a customer's need, in which they may not have the skills or expertise in providing for themselves. In essence, the business owner and what he or she can do for the client is the product they are selling, along with selling themselves (their character, reputation, and expertise).

For instance, if you offer business consulting services, your start-up costs are low; however, your upfront investment is the years of experience, education, and understanding of how a business works. These are the tools of the trade. If you decide to begin a property maintenance business, you will have to invest into lawn and building maintenance equipment, a service truck or two, and you may have to hire some help, depending on the job at hand.

Your services will be more targeted; as your goal is not to have the highest volume of clients, but the highest rate of quality client demand that results in higher revenue. A service-based business will focus on more personalized service and customer needs rather than the average cookie cutter mass produced model.

This type of model will allow for service based business owners to network with the most desired potential clientele. Service businesses must directly market to specific clients, and usually will prospect for customers inside a radius of the business's home location.

For example, a landscape and property maintenance business would not market to potential customers thousands of miles away, for the obvious logistical reasons that would make the endeavor unprofitable.

Your goal is to provide the highest quality of services to the highest quality of clients, in performing the most work for a smaller list of clients.

A service business can opt not to have a store front. Most service businesses which surround home services (a masonry, carpentry, or landscaping business) often operate out of their home, saving cost on a rental location. Other service based businesses like a hair salon or dry cleaner, rely on having a retailer location that allows for walk in foot traffic. A service business will focus on the need of the client, where the business is providing a service or skill set the potential client may not possess.

Because a service is intangible, it may be more difficult to connect and close deals with potential customers of your service if they cannot visualize the final result of the service you offer. Potential clients may be hesitant in purchasing a service even if their need of the service is great - if they cannot physically evaluate the outcome of their own buying decision.

A service-based business will experience a longer sales cycle because there are usually price and service negotiations, client contracts to review, and final review of the services provided, which in some cases will hold up final payment to the business owner.

Potential customers will rely on judgement calls when purchasing a service. Is the service provider trustworthy? Is the service provider of good character? Potential clients have a clear understanding that they cannot return a service once it's provided, so they are more cautious in making a decision. For this reason, most potential customers will desire to get the most dollar value out of the service they are purchasing, since the value proposition is beyond just the service itself. The consumer realizes that part of the value exchange is the experience of the journey through having the service provided to them.

Service-based businesses can overcome their unique challenges by offering the client a trial period for their services, giving the potential client an "out" if they are not happy with the service. This helps in removing some of the barriers during the negotiation of the purchase of a service.

Providing a list of referrals and references which the potential customer can call would be prudent. It would also be most helpful if the referrals and references are current clients of the business that have already purchased the same or similar services. The importance of this is to communicate confidence to the prospective client. Whether the sales representative (owner or employee) would be involved in providing the service, or other individuals are involved in providing a service, there is a quality connection of skills and service made through this business transaction.

A service is more challenging to promote, because there is nothing physical someone can hold in their hand. When marketing a service, it is more at the conceptual level of potential outcome and experience. When pitching a service, the business owner must convey the message and the value of the service they are going to provide, clearly, to the potential client.

The business owner must be able to be flexible and adjust their service offering to each client situation; no situations are alike. For example, if you are in the business of selling dry cleaning services, each individual client will have different needs and attention to the slightest of details will make all the difference in gaining future return business. The service industry relies on personal relationships and reliability.

The potential client must have total confidence and belief in your ability to deliver on your promises and skill sets. Therefore, it is necessary to provide your "why you are passionate about your business" and how that helps you deliver the best services available to your clients.

The start-up cost of service-based business is often much lower than that of a product-based retailer location. The type of services your business will offer will determine the type of investment you will need to make in order to fulfill customer demand. The startup cost of a service provider will also depend on the type of industry and service offered. In comparison, someone that wants to start up a landscape business will have far more up-front investment cost in equipment than someone that is providing consulting services to other businesses.

A service business usually has to invest more money into marketing and branding their own individual brand identity, because in many cases the business owner and their skill sets are the brand.

In either case, both a product- and/or service-based business boils down to a basic concept: you must have what someone else wants, which fills a need and provides an experience desired by the consumer.

You can assure yourself of one thing - there is no reward without some level of risk, regardless of product or service. All levels of business ventures require a cash investment, an investment of time, and an investment into knowledge of the industry by the business owner.

eye candy
857
Yes, we're
OPEN

– CHAPTER 8 –
Location, Location, Location; Where to Locate Your Business

Source: Before picking out a location to start your business, consider the many factors of its potential, as this issue is a key contributor to a business's success or failure.

Now that you have chosen the type of business to establish and the products and/or services you will be offering for sale, it is time to determine a location based on their own for your business. Most small business owners choose a location based on their own own perception of where they think the business might be a good fit. The reason for this is that many small business owners make this choice based on emotion.

Maybe you like a particular community or town, or maybe you spent your childhood there and the location is in close proximity to family and friends. Today business owners need to rely on data to help them make the best decision of where to locate their business, so that the business has the most optimum chance of succeeding.

The reality and hard disappointment is that your business will not survive if you are relying on only your friends and family to patron your enterprise. New relationships in a potential business location's community will be the driver to client acquisition; if you are specializing in a product or service, you will want to make sure the demographic of the potential consumers within that market region will be a good fit for your offering.

For example, if you are offering high end hand crafted furniture, you would want to locate your business in a town or community where the population would appreciate your value creation and have the disposable income to spend money on your goods or services. You might want to consider a store front location in a community or town surrounded by upper middle class home owners that appreciate hand crafted quality and are willing to spend the money on higher quality goods. This community may or may not be the same community or town in which you live. Your target market is one of the most important factors in deciding where your business will be located.

In addition to aligning your business products and services with the ideal clientele, you should consider additional contributing factors to how well your business may do in a specific location. Ask yourself, "Will this potential location transfer the message of my brand image?" Consumers need to identify your business from miles away, and in a quick moment of time. Does the location provide the best representation for your business? For instance, if you have a business that makes and sells clothing, would you rather have a storefront designed as a welcoming specialty boutique or would you rather locate in an office building where foot traffic may be limited?

You need to review your competition. Though it is true that your business is indirectly competing against every cash register in the world, on a local level you may want to examine the proximity and amount of competition. If you plan to open a barber shop or hair salon you will want to make sure the local area is not saturated with many of the same type of businesses. A saturation of the same type of business in a small local proximity means you will need to invest more money in customer outreach and marketing, a necessity most business owners find as only a luxury.

In turn you may want to consider indirect competition. These are businesses that may be in the same industry sector; however, they may not offer the exact same product lines or services that you do. A pharmacy and a natural food and health store would be considered indirect competition, as they might be able to complement each other. The pharmacy may offer health and wellness products via traditional medicine, while the natural foods and health store might carry a complete line of natural and holistic remedies and products. This is healthy competition because it offers the consumer real alternatives and choices on how to solve their health and wellness concerns.

You will also notice many businesses such as a dry cleaner, a bank, post office, pharmacy, and take-out restaurant in the same strip mall or plaza as a large grocery store. These are complementary businesses, as they may cater to the same customer multiple times and for different reasons, including the convenience of having this wide range of day-to -day customer services in one place.

If your business requires employees to help operate the day to day functions of the business, you might want to research the availability of qualified labor market candidates.

Many business owners complain that good help is hard to find; that may be due to the limited number of potential employees to choose from that are a proper fit for the business. If you do find the ideal employee, how far would they have to commute to your location? What perks or incentives would you have to offer employees for them to sacrifice time in the car in commuting to your business each day?

Many business owners think in two modes: the here and now, and the vision of twenty or thirty years from now. In the event your business is successful, a move to a larger location after you have sunk tens of thousands of dollars retrofitting your space today can be a costly mistake if you fail to initially plan your growth. If you think your business needs one thousand square feet today, the likelihood it will need to double its size in a year (if it is successful) is highly likely, especially if your business is retail- oriented.

A hardware store carries thousands of products and bar codes. Every local corner neighborhood hardware store I have visited in the past five years is starving for additional space, many with products being stacked to the ceiling. This is because new products for home use are constantly being offered.

The more product choices, the more brands your retail space offers, the more potential clients you may get to patron your store. Think in terms of three to five years down the road. If a space is too big, it is usually more negotiable to back out of space with a landlord than bump your business neighbor out of their current location so you can take over their space.

How close are you to your vendors and/or suppliers? If being within a range of distance to your vendors/or suppliers makes a difference to you, then this factor will also be a determining factor of where your business is located. If you use a third party to manufacturer your goods and need to have a close relationship with members of your supply chain daily, then your location should be within a day's drive of your suppliers. If your goods are delivered to you from a national warehouse, then the cost of delivery and freight may be a factor.

Safety should also be considered. Your employees would not favor working in a neighborhood that has a high crime rate. Your business could also fall victim to crime, as looters and thieves may see your retail location as a target for their caper. Rents in high crime areas may be less, but the risk may be higher.

Will the potential location offer enough parking for your customers and employees? Many towns have a requirement on how many parking spaces a business location must have based on the square footage the business occupies.

Traffic should also be examined. Is there enough vehicle traffic nearby that will provide exposure of your business to potential customers? Is the potential business location on a busy Main Street, or one located in the back ally of a down town cluster, blocked off by other industrial settings?

Before signing a lease, check with your local zoning and planning department to see if your type of business would be permissible at the potential business location. Not all commercial buildings are created equal. Some towns and cities have very strict zoning laws regulating where specific types of businesses may be located, as well as the permissible use of different types of commercial facilities.

Once you have conducted your preliminary research, it is time to take a hard look at cost. There is the upfront cost of renting a business location, such as the monthly rent/lease cost, property taxes and property maintenance fees.

There are indirect costs that can creep up over time and chew into a business owner's profits. These costs include the hidden cost of preparing the space for your business use. Most commercial space will need to be finished or renovated to accommodate the business purpose. Alterations are considered improvements to a property and will be taxed accordingly. Other taxes such as sales and use tax, payroll tax, and business income tax, will vary state to state.

Is your business location in an economic business development (EBD) zone? These zones are established by public policy and either receive tax break incentives for local job creation and/or has additional local licensing fees, which the business is required to pay; these licensing fees are sometimes used to aid in relief of the cost of workforce development and on the job training.

Minimum wage also varies from state to state. Many businesses may offer higher starting wages than minimum wage. Minimum wage is usually reserved for very low skilled jobs, sometimes fulfilled by either students or retired seniors that desire to work for part time income. The rise in minimum wage in some states make it impossible for some small business owners to hire help because the rate of minimum wage might be higher than the return on investment on the job tasks assigned to the employee.

Another vital piece of data every business owner needs to know regarding the town or region of their potential business is if the area is business friendly. This concept extends beyond just the potential customer. Having a clear understanding about how laws and regulations are imposed upon businesses, as well as how fees, penalties, and fines are assessed to businesses, is critical in knowing how much of your profits may be at risk to government representatives, eager to increase government revenue via enforcement actions.

A local or regional area may welcome small businesses to the table as the community governing body may consist of other local business owners. In a city where the majority of the businesses might be corporately owned and ran, local incentives and business practices may cater to the larger big box retailer. Many of these factors might not be as important to a virtual business, or a business that drop-ships its products to customers via third party, or to a medium-sized business that manufacturers and sells its goods to larger retailer-distributor partners. However, these factors will significantly impact the success of a locally owned restaurant, specialty retailer, or service business.

So, what states are the best and worst for your potential business location? There are several reports that vary in opinions of the "best" states for small business locations. I say if your business solves a problem and provides a common product or service critically needed by any community, and as long as you are customer service driven, then your business has a chance of being successful.

Forbes Magazine had issued a report about the top states for businesses. They took into consideration seven areas of interest when ranking all fifty states from the best to worst place to start a business. Factors included in their metrics of ranking were: the cost of doing business, labor market and supply, regulatory environment, economic climate, potential room for growth, and quality of life in relationship to the population of the state.

Utah was ranked number one in 2016 as the best state to begin a business with North Carolina following second and Nebraska falling into third on the list. Texas, Colorado, Virginia, Georgia, North Dakota, Washington and South Dakota rounded out the top ten states that best matched Forbes criteria.

According to Forbes, the worst states for a business were Hawaii, Rhode Island, Connecticut, Alabama, Vermont, New Mexico, Alaska, Mississippi, and Maine, with West Virginia topping the list. My home state of New Jersey ranked just outside the worst top ten states to do business.

The Business Insider took a slightly different view. In 2016, the Business Insider conducted a study which measured business conditions, which included the amount of start-up activity states reported, business survival rates, productivity based on Gross Domestic Product (GDP), employee availability, educational resources, business tax and cost of living.

Business Insider complied a ranking from worst to best places to begin a business. At the top of the worst states to establish a new business was Hawaii, which has some of the highest taxes in the country, highest cost of living, and limited potential work force. Second to Hawaii was the state of Maine. Neighboring Vermont swept third worst place to start a business, followed by Arkansas, Wisconsin, Maryland, South Carolina, Kentucky, Alabama, West Virginia, and Georgia. My home state of New Jersey fell to 39th on their list.

Business Insider gave glowing reports to Florida, Virginia, Missouri, Illinois, Utah, Delaware, and Texas, which ranked from tenth place to fourth place as some of the best states to begin a business in that order. Nevada was ranked third, as Alaska came in at the first runner-up bridesmaid position. Business Insider gave Wyoming the ranking as the best state to start and sustain a business.

But don't base your decisions solely on those statistics. One of the best ways to find out if a local town, city, county, or state is profitable for your business, is to go interview business owners in your industry sector on their experiences of why they like, or don't like, their business location.

You can ask them a series of questions such as: how long they have been in their location, the potential customer foot traffic that visits their store front, the cost of how much marketing they must invest in order to reach potential consumers, staff turn-over, regulatory climate, and other common business concerns important to your industry sector.

– CHAPTER 9 –

Finding the Money: Funding Your Small Business

Source: Business name, ✓ business product or service to be offered, check; ✓ business location selected, check; potential employees, check. Now all you need is the funding to upstart your idea. What kinds of financial resources are available for your small business venture start-up? Do you apply for grants or loans, or do you ask family and friends? Here we will look at various options for today's small business owner in funding their small business start-up.

One of the largest hurdles an entrepreneur will face in getting their business off the ground is funding. Many small business owners find it difficult to obtain the capital they need to finance their new business venture.

The good news is there are many options for capitalizing your small business venture. All you must do is research the opportunities and discover which finance options are best in line with the vision and growth strategy of your business.

There is an old philosophy about investing in one's self. Before you can ask others to invest in you, you must be willing to first invest in yourself. This is true for both money and time. There are a few reasons for this. There is an energy that is so powerful about one's own belief in themselves and about the venture they believe in, that when someone truly sacrifices everything (as in money and time), it sends a message to other potential lenders and/or investors. It says you have such high confidence and belief in your cause that you are willing to do what it takes to see your business be a success.

If you can self-fund your business it will eliminate the burden, stress and extra work that occurs in making a monthly payment to a funding institution or having extra measures needed to report to investors. There are several ways someone can self-fund their own business venture.

An individual can tap into their own personal savings account. The general rule of thumb is to reserve enough money from your personal savings to fund your own personal household expenses for six months to a year.

Most business owners are unable to take a draw against the business's profitability due to the lack of consistent cash flow in the early stages of start-up. If an individual has a stash of savings in a 401k or other type of retirement account, they may convert these investments into cash that can be applied to funding the new business venture. Be warned of any potential fees, penalties and taxes as a result from cashing in 401k accounts and retirement funds that have not yet matured.

There is newly found money when making a few lifestyle sacrifices. One must decide to live as frugal as possible while their new small business upstart begins to take hold. This means that you may want to consider cutting out some of the "extras" in your personal lifestyle. Subscription television (cable or satellite) can cost up to $150 per month; most business owners are home very little during the early growth of their business.

Plan to eat meals at home more often or bring your lunch from home. The average lunch out can cost between ten to fifteen dollars per day; preparing meals that can be reheated over several nights will save money and time.

Watching how you spend your disposable income will be more important than ever. All those impulse purchases of merchandise at the register of one's favorite retailer can eat away at cash better suited for building your own business. Make a list of items you need and stick to the list. Even dropping the temperature by a few degrees in the home can save a business owner a few dollars that can be allocated toward a business need. Every penny counts, and pennies add up to dollars, dollars that can help fund your business's utility or phone bill.

New business owners who are eager to get their enterprise off the ground will even consider turning personal assets to cash. There might be a few items around the house or in storage that you no longer treasure. This could range from paintings or collectable artwork, or maybe it's a collection of near rare hard to find antiques. These things can be sold and turned over for cash to help fund your new passion - your new business venture.

Maybe you have stocks, savings bonds, or other investments you would not mind parting with. Some households have a second or third car. You can sell the extra vehicle and apply the cash from the sale toward the business. If you are leasing or own a new car that is financed, you may want to consider trading in the vehicle for a good used car; you would have a lower monthly payment or even eliminate the payment and interest due.

A part-time job is another option in accumulating capital for your new business. An extra twenty hours of work a week could mean having another income that can be dedicated toward savings for up-starting the business.

Some people may have had a wealthy relative which was kind enough to include them in their will as part of their estate planning. An inheritance can be used as either start-up capital or for growth; just remember, such a gift is a one-time life event. The last option in self-funding a business is that a person may have the option to borrow from or even cash in their life insurance policy. Some policies will penalize the owner of the policy if it is cashed in before the policy has matured.

Boot strapping includes a series of economic practices initiating from existing resources. Examples can include self-funding a business, managing a business to have early cash flow, and a business's thriftiness.

Bootstrapping a business is necessary for most new small business owners until they have had an opportunity to prove the business model can turn out a profit. You may want to adjust your business service or product offering so that the sales cycle is shorter and the turnover of cash is quicker. Once the business has been able to show a consistency in its revenue, then it may be in a position to pitch for outside funding.

Not every business is a candidate for bootstrapping. Most service businesses which can operate from a home office can bootstrap their operations. Business categories of a business consulting firm, marketing/public relations business, an appliance repair business, a landscaping business, legal counsel, or accountant, are all businesses that offer services with little or no inventory.

Businesses that offer products are not in a strong position to bootstrap because they need funding for inventory. For the old saying goes, "an empty shelf never sells anything." Once your business is showing a profit consistently, then it can be taken seriously by potential lenders and/or investors.

There are a few grants available for small business owners. However, not everyone is eligible to apply or receive them. Most of the available business grants are tied to research and development (R&D). Some small businesses qualify for federal grants that conduct R&D; they are the Small Business Innovation Research grant, which is sponsored by the federal government programs, and the Small Business Technology Transfer.

Both programs require the small business ventures to meet specific qualifications, including but not limited to: being a US based company, American owned and operated, a for-profit business, limited to 500 employees or less, emloy a principle researcher employed by the company and to meet benchmarks of progress/growth to qualify for the next rounds of funding.

There are also specific category grants available, such as those to help promote and develop women business owned enterprises, veteran owned and operated business enterprises, minority business enterprises, and disabled or disadvantaged business enterprises.

Not only is grant money available, but also available are education, training, and mentorship programs, as well as fast track to set aside government sourcing-procurement opportunities. The US GSA, Department of Commerce, Department of Defense and multiple local and state agencies which manage spending of tax payer dollars on supporting the operations of government can all provide a schedule of available programs for these enterprises listed. The SBA offers a program specially tailored for veteran owned businesses. The Veterans Business Outreach Center Program was designed to provide training, mentorship and fast track veteran owned enterprises to become capitalized.

Another way to capitalize your business is to obtain a loan from family and friends. Keep in mind that just because they might be your friends or family, it is wise not to take advantage of their generosity. A loan after all is still a loan. Each "lender" should receive a return on their money (plus interest) for providing the use of their money for your venture.

You should also be very decisive about the use of their proceeds. Loans from family and friends should be short term, and invested into producing the actual product/inventory and/or service; assuring the lender they will get their money back when products/services are sold to customers.

Do not take more than what you absolutely need, for it is a good practice to limit the actual risk for some of your closest relationships. Be warned that if the business venture does not work out, you will still see your family and friends, so be careful not to put your closest valued relationships at risk. Money matters tend to always change the dynamic between friends and family members.

If you are fortunate enough to own your home or other valuable assets, you may qualify for a loan from a traditional lending institution, such as a bank or credit union. To get started with the initial funding for their business, some small business owners might refinance or mortgage their home, taking the cash value against the property and using the cash to jump start the business.

An alternative to mortgaging is a home equity loan, which is meant to be more short term, where money is provided against the home value, but it is not a long-term obligation.

Crowd funding sites such as Indiegogo and Kickstarter are excellent venues for a small business venture or a new entrepreneurial product idea to utilize. These two platforms also offer great opportunities for the pre-launch and marketing of book projects. When you sign up to offer your product, book, or idea on a crowdfunding site, you are encouraged to offer different levels of perks, including promotional products, flair, and the actual product or final book.

These sites do not promote the solicitation of investors. They are a platform for pre-selling your new market idea; offering perks and product discounts for the first market adopters of your idea. The key to a successful campaign is to tell your story, including the use of video and pictures. Then, you can market your program on multiple internet drivers such as social media platforms such as: You Tube, blogs, press releases and media, and radio.

Both Indiegogo and Kickstarter offer their services of collecting and distributing funds from individuals that sign up for perks, while charging a small fee for these services.

There may be a close friend, relative, or relationship with a person that shares the same passions and vision as you do, who would be interested in also starting a new business. They may not have as much time as you do to dedicate to the venture, however, they may have more financial resources they can put at risk. You may consider proposing to them the opportunity to become a business partner, where you both come to agreement on what each person will contribute to the business, and what responsibilities each party will be accountable for.

You will want to make sure that all the rules of engagement are spelled out between the parties. It is highly recommended that your business adopts a strong operating agreement, which is the governing document for your business. Sometimes business partners may decide to go their own seperate ways, and you want to be responsible in covering these important subjects, so there is no misunderstanding should a business partner decides to leave the business.

Your suppliers and vendors may also offer credit terms, allowing you to stock up on inventory while saving your cash until inventory is sold. Most businesses offer 30 day terms to other businesses which become regular suppliers of the new business. This gives you some time to turn over cash from inventory sold in a 30-day cycle, to repay the supplier.

Some suppliers will lend you the inventory on consignment. This means that inventory is provided to your business, and you are responsible for paying for the inventory once the goods have sold. To lessen the liability of owing suppliers for inventory not yet in the hands of the customer, you may want to research consignment terms.

Not all suppliers offer these terms. Most new, smaller, independent suppliers might offer consignment terms if they are just getting started themselves. Consignment terms provide an opportunity for two new businesses to go to market, while building a long-term relationship.

If you know that you will be paid by your clients withen thirty days, then credit cards are a good alternative for very short-term financing of your business. Some cards offer no interest or low interest for new businesses to gain future ongoing business. Some credit cards offer cash back or points for using the credit card much the same as a debit card. A business can benefit from using credit cards to pay its bills, if it is receiving a cash back bonus. You must pay credit card balances on time or your business will be subject to losing all of the benefits the card provides. Having a positive credit rating with credit cards, will help the business build its credit score, so that in the future, if you choose to get a loan or larger line of credit, the business would be deemed credit worthy.

There are alternatives to hard money when making transactions from one business to another. Businesses can barter services or products for other services or products they may need in building their business, allowing the business to conserve its hard cash for other expenses. For instance if a hardware store business needs a sign for their storefront and the sign maker needs materials to build and install signs, the two businesses can trade a sign in exchange for a store credit for hardware inventory.

There are business barter platforms springing up as barter has become a popular way to obtain your business needs without laying out the cash from the register. One barter platform that is exceeding the rest is Badger Barter, located throughout the Sun Prairie and Madison, Wisconsin business community.

Badger Barter uses barter credits for trading between businesses; a business can use their earned barter at other businesses, freeing up the traditional direct barter to barter commitment. New businesses can qualify for a line of credit, allowing them to use barter credits in the very beginning of launching their business. Once the business is on its feet, it would then repay the barter credits to the barter system. Most businesses offer a discount to other barter members within the Badger Barter program. It's also a way to attract new business to your door, as some clients may only patron businesses that are a part of the barter network.

Another option worth considering is that a business can get a loan against its accounts receivables. Factoring loans are short term commitments, where specialty lenders will provide up to 80% of the invoice amount to your business. They will advance you the cash against your invoice, then proceed to take over the collection process from your business and client. Once they have collected the invoice balance due from the client, the remaining 20% is split between you and the factoring lender, who charges a small fee for the loan and their collection services.

Most factoring loan terms are 90 to 120 days until maturity date and will charge up to 8% for their services. Another type of factoring lending is a business cash advance, where the lender is buying your current and future accounts receivables. These types of loans will require a daily draw from your business bank account. Between fees and the advance, you can expect to pay as high as 30% for these kinds of factoring arrangements.

If your small business value proposition is considered a market disruptor, your business may qualify to be part of a business incubator group. These groups allow for many small business ideas to share space in a flex business center or research center as the business gets off the ground. A business incubator can be beneficial for a tech start up, where retail space is not required. Business incubators are platforms where the idea is carried into the concept stage with the hopes of developing a business model. Usually business incubators prioritize its efforts on developing the innovation.

A business accelerator business center offers some of the same services as the business incubator group with a major distinction that the business accelerator project is now market ready, and teams up the founder or entrepreneur with mentors, outside management assistance, and potential venture capital groups.

While the business accelerator is focused on actual business development, the concept transfers into becoming a market-ready product. These business centers can be found at Universities, through the US SBA programs, and/or even venture capital groups will sponsor a business accelerator center. In some cases where the business model advances, capital is provided and costs are shared.

Some towns and states offer new businesses a series of tax credits in exchange for meeting criteria for a specific tax credit. Some examples of tax credits include the Research and Development tax credit. This program allows for innovative businesses to utilize a tax credit reward and other tax benefits for investing business dollars toward research and development projects that result in the creation of jobs. Some new businesses can take advantage of a property tax credit if they assume the responsibility of purchasing a redevelopment property or brownfield and remediate the property for commercial use.

Property tax credits are also available in some states if a new business hires a minimum of new or additional staff, and keep new employees employed for a minimum term. To get a sample of what some states offer, one can look to the Start Up New York Program, which offers a host of tax credits to qualified businesses. Money saved on taxes is money that a business owner can allocate toward other business needs, like marketing, advertising, or inventory.

The last place to find money is by way of an angel investor or venture capital group. These two types of investing groups look for opportunities where they will get a piece of the new business in turn for their money, experience, connections, relationships, and mentorship.

Most angel or venture capital investor groups will usually review a business that has developed a new product or technology that has large market growth opportunities. It is rare that an angel or venture capital investor group will invest into a small business, unless that small business has something so unique it can be taken to market beyond the localized area. One platform that has brought entrepreneurs and investors together is Funding Post (FundingPost.com). This forum helps educate entrepreneurs how to pitch their idea to potential angel and venture capital groups, while matching potential investor groups to specific industry space start-ups.

Before you consider the outside investor route, you will want to consult with an attorney that specializes in securities laws, since each state has different criteria on how a business may offer investment in their company.

Before making any financial decisions, you may want to consult with a financial planner and your own financial advisor about the possible options and risk when liquidating your own personal assets or leveraging your assets to acquire a loan. The money is there; you just have to find it.

– CHAPTER 10 –

Establishing the Governance of your Business

Source: Establishing the rules of engagement is one of the most critical steps in protecting the legacy of one's business from potential risk. To set the tone of the law of the land for your new venture, you must have an effective operating agreement or company charter. This becomes the place of reference when it's time to deal with a dispute between business partners, or provide the road map on how to handle financial matters.

Having an operating agreement can either save or cost your business financial resources. Other guidelines and standards will also allow management to better grow your business.

In the initial hustle and bustle of establishing a new small business venture, I have found that most small business owners overlook the importance of setting up rules and standards by which their business is to be governed. Then later, because the rule of law of the business was overlooked or never formally established, they are forced to face challenges that put the business at risk.

I have seen several small businesses face serious consequences, including litigation involving a business partner, employee disputes, and changes in relationships with vendors, all because they did not have key agreements and elements in place.

Every business start-up enterprise has an opportunity to minimize further risk by establishing key agreements in the very beginning. It does not matter how well you know your business partner, or that your investor is a family member; when money and time is involved, each person has a set of expectations that may not be as clearly expressed as they should. Many issues and concerns can be addressed for business owner(s), investor(s), employees, vendors, and even third parties and clients, through a number of governing tools.

Most small businesses are either a sole proprietorship or are a limited liability company. In these cases, a document known as an Operating Agreement, acts as the business's decree on how many operational and executive decisions can be made, how profits and/or losses are distributed to business partners or members of the LLC, and dissolution of the business.

Some of the most effective Operating Agreements have provisions that address the following areas: assignment of managers (directors); recognition of the capital infusion by each member or business owner; allocation of the percentage of ownership to each owner-investor; establishment of rules on how to treat profits/losses and the treatment of cash flows; members meetings, rights, and voting procedures; accountability; transparency; member-manager compensation for their services provided within operating the business; and additional provisions on how to handle a member or business partner's request to leave or exit the business. These are key areas of concerns that can make or break a business.

Having an effective Operating Agreement will help mediate and mitigate disagreements between business partners. Each owner or partner, and/or member must agree to each term and condition within the Operating Agreement as well as abide by upholding the standards of conduct spelled out in this type of document. In essence, the Operating Agreement becomes the law of the land for that business entity.

Once an Operating Agreement is signed by all owners, managers and members of that business, it should be notarized and filed with the business entity's state of jurisdiction, with the Office of the Secretary of State. In the event of a dispute, the rule of law for that business can be recognized when issues may result in having to litigate in Court.

The devil is in the details of an Operating Agreement. A business partner (or partners) who is not fully honest about their long-term intentions, or by counsel of each business partner, can poison a business. To avoid or prevent this, there are a few critical areas of an Operating Agreement any business owner should take notice of.

When it comes to changing the terms and conditions of an operating agreement, the standard is the party that holds 51% stake of the business entity or more can change the operating agreement at any time. To avert this catastrophic clause, two business partners can agree that it takes 85% of the voting members to change the agreement. This means that if one business partner owns 49% and the other owns 51%, neither business partner can change the rule of governance without consent or vote of the other party.

Another area to focus on within the Operating Agreement is how to treat cash, profits and losses. You and your business partner should clearly communicate your expectation on how distribution will occur in these areas. Most businesses will issue a quarterly distribution. Usually at the time of filing taxes for the business, losses are distributed equally to individual members based on the amount of initial investment each member contributed to the business. You may want to consider setting aside a cash allocation for the business so it has its own resources for paying taxes, liabilities, or for future growth funding needs.

An Operating Agreement should have clauses on how to discipline a member or manager that has committed an act against the business, one so harmful that it puts the business in jeopardy of dissolving. Also, if a business partner decides they no longer wish to continue with the business, (abruptly leaving another business partner with a host of liabilities) what terms and conditions are in place to protect the other members and business owners from these kinds of early exit decisions? An operating agreement can spell out the step by step process and conditions by which a member may exit the business, without being a detriment to the remaining business owners.

What if you are a sole proprietor? Do you need an Operating Agreement? The answer is yes and here is why. What if down the road your business experiences a change in circumstances that leaves you having to explore the option of partnering up with an investor or operational business partner? You want to have a rule of governance in place that spells out the very terms of that business's ongoing policy so the new business partner cannot impose any new self-rule or put at risk your previous years' worth of financial investment and sweat equity.

A company charter is reserved for corporations; for companies structured as an "S" or "C" corporation. Usually, in the state in which a corporation is established, there is already an established standard charter which provides the "shareholder(s)" of that corporation rights afforded to them under the rule of state law. These chartered rights cannot be amended; however, a company can opt to adopt additional rules to a charter. Also, a corporation has other tools available to them in establishing governance.

A company can require its shareholders and executives to sign and abide by a Code of Ethics.

Employees can be required to read and abide by the rules of the company's employee handbook. Independent contractors who are not direct employees of the company and/or vendors can be held to a series of established standards as the company has the freedom to establish policy that is in the best interest of the company and its shareholders.

Much the same as having standards for each business partner to follow, there also needs to be rules and guidelines for your employees. A company-employee handbook will offer the ground rules for employees, informing them about the business's expected conduct of each employee.

A company-employee handbook provides guidelines in areas such as dress code, corporate company policy, employee-employer rights, employee privileges, perks, and other metrics of standards that are aimed at helping the employee become the best they can at their role within the company.

A well thought out comprehensive company-employee handbook can help a business avoid disagreements with employees on issues that arise from the employee's expectations from the business, as well as the business's expectations from the employee. Each state has some differences on the rule of labor laws, which should also be incorporated into the company-employee handbook. Most company-employee handbooks are standardized for small businesses, and can be obtained via a human resource consulting company.

When a business is a boutique or specializes in a specific area of practice, some additional measures should be considered. For instance, if your business has sensitive information about its clients, how is their data and privacy assured by the businesses employee? If your business deals with technology or proprietary intellectual property, what clauses are in place to protect the business and/or the employee in regards to intellectual property secrets?

Within the company-employee handbook, you can also inform employees about the company's hiring and promotion practices, so each employee has a clear understanding of how the company determines employee advancement. As a small business that, in some cases may only have one or two employees aside from the business owner, a company-employee handbook may not cover every detail; however, if you aspire for your small business to grow beyond Main Street into a medium size business enterprise, your company-employee handbook needs to cover as many areas of current and future employee-employer concerns, so the stage of expectations is established to foster the growth of your labor force.

Your relationships with suppliers and vendors are part of the life blood of your business. As each business deals with mounting compliances required by their state, small businesses need to consider how these regulations will affect their supply chain. Some states require compliance and accounting of environmental footprints of a supply chain, which is a reverse logistics policy. Here, each part of a small business's line of vendors can be held equally responsible to standards and guidelines as the small business is providing products and services to the public.

Businesses that supply local and state government agencies with goods and/or services, have additional burdens in which the small business must filter down requirements to their suppliers. One of these initiatives is a "Made in the USA policy," where the local or state agency requires local businesses that sell to government, only sell products that are originated in the United States.

You can place other requirements on your vendors and suppliers that best suit your businesses core values. If you use a lot of copy paper, and you believe the health and future of the environment to be important, you can require your vendor to supply you with materials that are made from recycled paper. If you have specific delivery times in which you accept deliveries from vendors at your business, you can notify them of the exact dates and times that your staff is available to accept deliveries from vendors. No matter the policy, your business may issue to your vendors a vendor a list of required policies they must follow that best suits your business's needs. Some vendors or suppliers have specific criteria a small business must comply with. Be sure to read the fine print. Some of these policies are designed to penalize a small business that does not fit the standard of the vendor's expectations.

There are several additional common agreements a small business may consider as part of its rule of governance, with the purpose of protecting its interest. A small business might sanction independent sales representatives to help the business sell its products and/or services. An independent sales representative agreement will provide both the company, and the contracted sales agent, a set of parameters of what each party is responsible for, while also providing to the sales representative information on how to best represent the businesses' product/service being offered. Often sales commissions and payment details are included in these agreements.

Another agreement a business may find helpful is a code of ethics. A code of ethics might cover rules and guidelines, not necessarily provided by local or state law; however, it is important to the business and business owner. Most of the items contained in a code of ethics are related to the morality and core values of the leadership of the company. Within the business's code of ethics, extra standards in holding accountable an employee or executive to either behaviors or decisions, while not unlawful, are still detrimental to the business, and can be highly effective in deterring such types of behaviors.

The larger your vision for your business operation, the more time you will want to devote to establishing agreements, rules of governance, guidelines and company policies, to assure the business can function, even when challenges from within arise. It is also wise to consult with legal counsel, an accountant, and a human resource specialist, so that you can take into consideration the local and state laws and protections as part of your overall agreements.

Section III:
Working in Your Business

eye candy
Yes, we're
OPEN

– CHAPTER 11 –

Business Cost versus Investment

Source: We take a look at the most common business expenses and determine whether they are a cost or an investment; explaining the difference.

The Small Business Administration estimates that nearly half of all new businesses fail and disappear in the first five years of operation. One of the key reasons for this unfortunate statistic is that the majority of businesses are underfunded, and do not have enough cash on hand to pay for operational expenses during lean times. If your business is one of the more fortunate stories, congratulations, you survived the statistics; however, you might still be operating on a shoe string because cash is limited.

I have seen many businesses in this condition when they are operating with very limited cash; Business owners will often say they cannot afford to spend money, whether it be on marketing and advertising, new equipment, or even on hiring new employees. Managing cash can be a balancing act. There is the old saying, "you must spend money to make money". So, when it is safe to spend money as a small business?

When allocating valuable financial resources as a small business, one must ask, "What is my return on investment on spending the money?"

First, you must determine whether the business expense is an investment or a cost. Most business costs are either fixed expenses such as rent for a storefront, or cash spent on inventory or labor, all of which may be at risk if the product or service never sells.

A business may spend cash on services associated with marketing and/or advertising, which should be viewed as a long term investment, because they help generate leads which eventually lead to sales; sales that may have never occurred if the advertising effort was not done.

Let's take a closer look at some of these factors.

Operational necessities that may not provide a return on investment should be treated as a cost. The basics such as an office or storefront location, phone, and basic website, should be treated as costs. These are expenses that are a must if you provide a service and/or product, and depend on foot traffic for sales.

If you offer "free delivery" such as a pizza parlor or dry cleaning service, there is a cost in providing the service of the delivery such as the vehicle, a driver, vehicle maintenance, insurance, and fuel cost. Other examples of hard cost which may be indirect to providing your product or services include, but not limited to, the cost of taxes, cost of licensing and permits, accounting and legal services, all which require a business to spend money.

Some expenses are perceived as costs, but should be categorized as an investment. One of the largest investments any business can make is in its employees. Yes, an investment into people will help grow your business.

In the book, Profit at the Bottom of the Ladder; Creating Value by Investing in Your Workforce, the author, Jody Heymann, explains how a company benefits by offering additional skills training to employees at the expense of the business.

"These companies have been profitable for their owners and shareholders, while being profitable for their employees, because they have been profitable for their employees," writes Heymann,

"Employees determine 90% of most businesses' profitability."

Other studies have found when employers recognize the needs of their employees, employees become less worrisome of their own issues in the workplace and more productive and profitable for the business in which they are employed.

Another area which most small business owners tend not to recognize as an investment is marketing and advertising.

Marketing includes the practice of branding, market capability research, choosing the appropriate demographic audience and geographic fit for their business, and lead generation. Most marketing programs will determine the most effective advertising approaches for a business to be noticed by potential customers.

A program that employs both a marketing plan and targeted advertising campaign is the best use of cash when trying to get your business noticed. Most small businesses will allocate a very small budget in this area, and expect advertising to instantly provide a return of big dollars in sales from the first ad placement out.

Marketing and advertising is a long term engagement and should be treated as a long term investment. The more consistent and specific the effort, the more effective the return on investment will be. Most successful businesses will spend 20% of all of their working capital on marketing and advertising; however, many small business owners hesitate on spending cash on marketing and advertising, thinking they cannot afford it, or it is wasteful.

The truth is, you cannot afford <u>not</u> to advertise. People will usually patron a business that is at the top of their mind. If you are not in front of your potential customer, then you do not exist to them.

Most small businesses also hesitate to implement systems or technology that will save them time; processes that may automate business functions. Time is money, and most small businesses in America have less than five employees. It is important to maximize use of an employee's time. There are many information technologies, software systems, and communication platforms that can help manage staff and tasks, minimizing or even eliminating some cost.

Should you rent, lease, or purchase your location? It depends. In some cases, it is more advantageous to the business owner to rent or lease their location, both of which are tax deductible expenses.

But when it is more expensive to rent and cheaper to own the physical location, a business owner may want to consider making the investment into owning the building versus renting it. Owning the business location can be a business in itself and a smart investment. The building might be a multiple unit building that provides rental income which can be valuable for offsetting costs associated with the upkeep of the building.

You must also consider the age old reminder, "location, location, location" in evaluating whether spending your cash on a building is a smart investment. Your location itself is an investment. The closer you are to your ideal clientele, the more probable that you will be be noticed by that targeted audience.

Investing in your small business will always be a risk. Risk is limited by having a sound understanding of the possible returns on your risk. Setting realistic expectations on desired results will help develop a discipline on how you spend your cash.

The age old saying, "you must spend money to make money," is true; however, you can determine the best use of that cash by having a clear understanding of expense as an investment (that will help grow the business) or as a cost (just a part of doing business).

The evaluation of your expenses as either a cost or an investment will aid in curbing wasteful spending.

– CHAPTER 12 –

Effective Supply Chain Management Practices for Your Small Business

Source: Every Small Business has needs as a part of doing business: general operations; marketing cost; inventory or cost of goods sold; cost of compliance; and the management of all of the suppliers for their business needs. Here are some practices that allow for better supply chain management.

The management process may be a bit overwhelming at times, and if left unchecked, vendors and suppliers may overstep their bounds, taking advantage of the small business. Here are a few tips on how to establish an effective vendor/ supply chain management system for your small business.

The first area you should explore is properly classifying each vendor. Each vendor and/or supplier has a classification and a category. It does not matter if you are a product based business (with a storefront) or only offer services (like a legal practice); most small businesses will have the following categories: vendors-suppliers which support **operations** (location-rent, phone, utilities, waste disposal, location maintenance, company vehicles if any); **employees-human resources** (including independent contractors); **marketing** (including but not limited to website, print materials, advertising, signage); **cost of goods sold or inventory** (including, but not limited to, any other entity responsible for your actual product or service being supplied or manufactured); and **professional services** (this would be your attorney, accountant, advisors, etc.). By putting each vendor into a category, it will aid you in your management process of your suppliers.

Another way to streamline your supply chain is to separate each vendor by their preferred payment method. Most businesses are now accepting multiple payment methods, and some vendors and suppliers have specific paying methods they accept; some will accept only traditional forms of payment while some suppliers may be part of a barter network.

This is important because if you need to conserve cash, you may reach for vendors whom accept either barter and/or crypto-currency first. It is wise to have a few possible back-up vendors in each category, and to have those that accept different forms of payment (in case you get short on cash and need things for your business).

Create a detailed, yet manageable, Supply Chain Criteria. Having a Vendor Supply Chain Kit for your business is a great way to keep all of your vendors/suppliers on point. If you have specific requirements in your administrative process on how to treat your vendors and the documents you need to have on file from them, you can create a kit that includes all of the required documents you must have on file, in order to issue 1099's. these would include the vendor supplier agreement and/or consulting contract between the two parties and any other policies you require your vendors/suppliers to follow. In turn, any payment term sheets or vendor policies should also be in your copy of this kit. Having these documents available in a dispute can quickly resolve issues.

Establish a competitive bid process for your vendors. In order to get the most for your money, you should have on file a procedure of a bid process for vendors to compete for your business. In some business categories, businesses knowing they have to compete may offer more, including perks and extras; this may result in even better payment terms.

You will need to "spell out" the specific instructions on how you will vet each potential vendor/supplier, what you expect from them, the number of units or widgets you desire, and the expected time of delivery.

Automate Your Supply Chain. Most large companies utilize Electronic Data Interchange or EDI, systems and software to manage just in time inventory controls and receiving/ordering of goods from vendors. This software is an investment; however it cuts down on your need for redundant order takers. You can have just one individual processing your entire purchasing, shipping and receiving, and payment infrastructure using a trusted EDI package.

Get your quality control policies in place for vendor product and/or service. Have expectations and policies in place that can aid in measuring quality control of the product or service provided. Have a system of accountability and consequences in place for cases of sub-par product or service. This will eliminate waste and undue burdens of vendor mistakes. Policies aimed at handling a situation can help your business quickly mitigate an issue with a vendor.

Conduct a yearly review process. Annually, meet face to face with every vendor in your supply chain process. This gives you an opportunity to set goals and expectations as your business grows. In addition, you can re-negotiate terms and conditions after developing a relationship and track record. This also allows you to grade your vendors and decide whether or not to continue the relationship. If market place trends change, you can negotiate better terms or pricing at this meeting.

When vetting potential vendors and suppliers, request samples, references, and case studies. Prior to contracting a vendor, you should see if they can handle the task. Ask for a test batch of product or have fact checked with a number of referrals when you are about to commit to a large dollar amount product order or services.

Some of your vendors may have better "niche" areas than others; you will want to offer the right job to the right vendor, saving you money, time, and disappointment . Only you know what you want, so choose the right candidates based on your vision, business needs, and the price you are willing to invest into those needs.

eye candy
857
Yes, we're
OPEN

– CHAPTER 13 –
Cost Effective Small Business Strategies

Source: Small Business Strategies that work, are open for consideration by the Small Business Owner/Operator and/or Family Owned Business Organization, while aimed to provide an advantage in positioning small business in front of their desired audience.

Small Businesses need every advantage available to them. Across America, family owned small businesses have struggled with the invasion of big box retailers whom have strategically placed their store locations to purposefully draw audiences of consumers away from Main Street.

So how does a Small Business Compete against this kind of capitalism?

There are three areas of competency that Small Businesses can incorporate into their business strategy; these are cost effective and keep small business owners visible to their potential customer audience.

Relationship building is key to all the moving parts of your business. Small Businesses are more reliant on client relationships than ever before.

Common bonds and a solid presence in the community provide strategic advantages for small businesses. The business owner can personally engage with clients. If your product and/or service are for a commercial business to business offering, joining a local chamber of commerce and/or a local business barter exchange will enable you to directly meet with decision makers of your ideal clientele.

Your main investment is your time, in networking, and in getting to know your potential client. You must be "out in front" of your potential or current client and stay out in front. If you cannot be seen, people will think you do not exist. It is not enough to be listed on a directory and hope the phone will ring; you must extend the olive branch and take a sincere interest in the other party's business growth needs, goals, and vision.

When these types of bonds are established, you will be surprised by how partnerships and alliances are formed. One example of these types of mutually beneficial alliances might exist between a graphic artist/web design/marketing firm and a company that makes signs for businesses and letters vehicles. Initially, they may seem like competitors, but both have their niche offering. When a complete business marketing-and-advertising plan is put into action, each business benefits from doing business with the client by focusing on their niche. These types of situations illustrate referrals that generate income.

Embrace educational opportunities. One of the best ways to establish yourself as a local expert is to host a local seminar on subject matter related to your industry. For example if you own a local senior health care nursing home facility, and you wish to indirectly sell your facility's services to potential consumers, you could host a seminar about elder care, and how to properly determine which type of facility will suit your loved one's needs.

Such a seminar can be hosted at the local library, firehouse, or community recreational center. Usually you can borrow the space for a small donation. Within an hour you can demonstrate that you are the local expert folks should seek out for advice. Your expertise will speak for itself, resulting in client flow.

Getting involved in a local educational program can also help a business grow. You can volunteer to be a mentor in a business or trade- related educational enrichment program at your local high school or college. Your contribution of sharing knowledge with students does not go unnoticed; parents of the students, other faculty, and even local media, will recognize your donation of your expertise in uplifting the future workforce.

Programs like Distributive Education Clubs of America (DECA) and Future Business Leaders of America (FBLA) are student education enrichment programs in which students take an active role in understanding and practicing many facets of business, corporate, and industry standards.

Many of these student programs offer work study situations, in which students obtain gainful employment at a local merchant, that enables them to practice their class room learning in a real-life work situation. These programs yield student employees with a higher understanding of the importance of business operations, marketing, industry standards, and business ethics. If you are in search of student or part-time help, this is a great place to recruit future employees.

Consider getting involved in a non-profit community cause or fundraisers. There is significant value in lending a hand and/or some resources to local community causes. Cause marketing is a growing phenomenon that is accelerating among small to medium size businesses and companies. A local business can donate their space for just a few hours to host a local fund drive or an event that allows for donations to be collected.

For example, a hair salon may choose to help a local food bank and, for a designated time during business hours (usually 2 to 4 hours) a donation is made to the food bank out of all of your sales for that specific duration. In addition, you could take up a collection of food for the food bank. Since you are providing a local public service that benefits a local non-profit organization, news media and radio stations will sometimes provide free air time.

Once the general public is in your door, you can provide them with some take away information and promotional offers. This form of good will can get you mentioned in newspaper articles; the non-profit community cause would most likely provide a public recognition of your service. These types of community good will create "top of the mind" awareness with local audiences.

Some companies even allocate a portion of their profits to non-profit community causes. For instance, the product Extreme Kleaner (an environmentally friendly non-toxic biodegradable multi-purpose cleaner-degreaser) donates a portion of every product sale back into a fund to assist disabled and/or homeless Veterans; STEM Education; and/or the Arts. Consumers know that their purchase is making a difference in someone's life aside from just making a company profit. This has aided in this product's sales to skyrocket. Look to adopt cause marketing as part of your business strategy.

eye candy
Yes, we're
OPEN

– CHAPTER 14 –

Suggested Systems Integration for Small Business

Source: Most small businesses are owner-operated or operate with only a few employees. So how does a small business owner effectively handle many of the required tasks in order to stay in compliance, be profitable, and on top of customer request? Here we will review a number of systems and programs a small business can consider for their operations.

Gone are the days of tracking your business's transactions using just a paper accounting ledger. As businesses and their suppliers become more intertwined, small businesses are finding themselves in an awkward place. Yet, the number of dollars saved (not lost) by having to conduct a routine physical inventory count or to reverse paper trails on business spending needs, can help pay for integrated systems over time.

Today, we live in such a fast-paced society, businesses now demand information to be at the fingertips of a business owner, either when handling an order with a supplier, calculating payroll and taxes, or even when managing customer service. Not every small business management software solution is applicable to every small business; however, there are some core functions in which software can help every business. Let's look at these systems and why they are beneficial for a small business to consider.

Every small business needs a way to track its financial transactions beyond the cash register. There are several software programs that earned attention since they bundle a number of platforms and areas of accounting into one integrated system. The most common and widely recommended business accounting program is Quick Books.

Quick Books platforms range from packages that service a small at-home business (which may have fewer accounting concerns) to the Quick Books Enterprise platform, designed to accommodate an entrepreneur with a growing business concern. This package includes employees, suppliers, and inventory, as well as payables and receivables. Quick Books has developed their packages to fit the business enterprise regardless of the scale and size of small to medium size businesses.

All your day-to-day accounting functions for your business can be handled by the Quick Books system by integrating client-customer information, supplier information, tax accounting, and operational costs. This program can enable you to also issue invoices, receipts, and checks. Quick Books offers more support and training tools than most other accounting programs for small business owners. Quick Books can be hosted on a computer or the cloud, allowing for a small business owner to "farm out" bookkeeping tasks to third parties.

Quick Books have made their platforms mobile friendly; no matter where the business owner is, they can take care of transactions on the go. Quick Books offers their programs and services for as little as $5 per month and scaling to $199 per month, depending on your business enterprise needs.

When a business transitions their accounting measures from a paper process to a digital platform, a business can expect to increase their productivity. Business owners can use a plug-and-play system like Quick Books, and can free up time for more important business functions. Money will be saved, including business costs on accounting, since the system can help better manage costs, accounts payable deadlines and discounts. The business owner might be more inclined to personally handle their accounting instead of outsourcing this task.

Digital accounting will provide for more accurate information and present that information in a series of reports, available at the time of preparing and reporting business taxes. The business owner has the extra level of comfort that their business's information is now more secure than ledger books that once laid around their office or store.

Partnered with an accounting system, every business owner with employees needs an integrated payroll system. These payroll systems are designed to automatically calculate and deduct employee payroll taxes and employer contributions, based on each employee's level of salary-wages and dependent declaration.

Intuit recently partnered with Quick Books so that a small business can easily integrate their employee payroll tax reporting as one of the functions of their standard accounting procedures. Pricing for Intuit varies, based on the number of employees. However, Intuit allows a business to subscribe to services as the business either grows or shrinks. Intuit is for the business owner that likes to be involved in all aspects of running their business.

The business owner can delegate payroll to a third party. Companies such as Pay Chex and ADP are just two examples of large payroll services that can be considered by a small business owner if they choose not to manage their own payroll system.

Business Daily News ranked the top five rated payroll systems for small business, ranking Intuit the best small business payroll solution.

For business owners that have an S or C corporation, and receive their benefits from the profits of the business, Gusto is recommended as the system of choice.

For the single operator, with limited financial transactions, such as those in service based businesses, On

Pay might be the better system for your payroll reporting needs.

If you manage your household or property like it's a business, and you have many workers around your home such as a grounds keeper, visiting nurse, nanny, or personal chef, the Sure Payroll system has you covered. Business Daily News reviewed several factors in rating each payroll system; including cost, tax services provided, ease of use, system integration, mobile access, and support.

In setting up any payroll system, it is important to document your small business' steps. First you must obtain an Employer Identification Number (EIN) from the IRS. This will be issued when filing for corporate identity, tax id number, and trade name. Check to see if your state or county require additional business registrations, since each state's requirements and payroll tax withholdings vary. All employees, upon their acceptance of employment, must fill a out a form providing the small business with personal information related to how they will be declaring their personal income with the IRS.

A small business owner needs to understand the difference between hiring an independent contractor or a direct employee. This makes all the difference in how the small business treats payroll and payroll tax accounting. Once a payroll system is chosen, keep accurate records and files on hand in case of an audit and/or when the business needs to report and file payroll taxes.

Electronic Data Interchange (EDI) is a software system which integrates communications between vendors, customers, and one's business; this includes the functions of accounting and inventory systems in one platform, allowing for expediency of order fulfillment to customers that require complete transparency.

EDI systems offer a host of business-to-business compliance integration, developed and aimed to increase quality control and efficiency. Companies such as ACE Hardware require its vendors and hardware store owners to use EDI; this enables ACE corporate to better manage warehouse inventory levels, payments to vendors, and distribution of goods to local ACE Hardware stores.

EDI has become the standard in the retail industry. Locally owned retailer locations such as an auto parts store or food market might have hundreds or even thousands of products on their shelves. When these stores re-order merchandise from suppliers and distributors, EDI helps verify with the warehouse products that are in stock and ready for delivery.

In turn, EDI will notify a vendor to automatically send the next round of goods to the warehouse as inventory levels become low. EDI will also be used to manage payments, rebates, and coupons between stores, warehouses and vendors. If your business is a high-volume retailer location, chances are, EDI will be required as part of your store's serviceability.

Retailer-based businesses and some service businesses carry several inventories, which must be managed. In some cases, a business may be a retailer and offer services whose inventory is segmented into separate categories. A hair salon may carry product for sale at a retail counter, and they might have inventory which is required to provide their services. An inventory control system can be helpful. There are a few different types of widely used inventory control systems.

The Perpetual Inventory Control System allows for new inventory to be entered into a business's system on a regular basis. Once inventory is sold or used, the system updates itself, providing for accurate up to date inventory levels in real time. The perpetual system provides sales data; a business owner can track trends of products that sell the quickest, versus product that may sit for a while. These systems do have some room for error, therefore, it is wise for a business to physically count inventory and match the results against the system's account.

The periodic inventory system is a lesser involved inventory control system. It works, based on taking a "snap shot" of all products in inventory at set periods of time. This system will only recalculate inventory levels on the pre-determined benchmarks (monthly, quarterly, or yearly), a benefit to a business if they do not sell as much inventory as a retailer business would. This system is cost effective; however, it does have its drawbacks. If a business needs to have a better understanding of inventory levels on a daily basis, the periodic inventory system lacks the intelligence to provide data on demand.

The third small business inventory control option is called the manual method; the business owner utilizes a series of spreadsheets and personally enters the data of specific inventory sold or used internally by their business. Columns and categories are used for each of the most important information about the inventory, including, but not limited to, the product's bar code, size and dimensions, expected shelf life, number of units, and location of the inventory. This type of inventory tracking must be updated manually, and if the business owner fails to update the information, their calculations will be wrong. This system has very little or no cost but that of the business owner's time.

Not every business owner can dedicate their time to managing every social media platform available. It is crucial for local small businesses to be engaged in social media and employ social media marketing as part of their customer outreach; however, there are over a dozen highly used social media platforms which connect the small business with new potential customers. They are include, but are not limited to, Facebook, Google Plus, Twitter, YouTube, Pinterest, Instagram, Linked In, My Space (yes, some people still use it), Tumblr, VK, Flickr, and Meetup. It can be time consuming and laborious for a business owner to have to separately repost daily marketing content to each of these sites.

New social media dashboard tools, designed to help save time and manage content, have been a blessing for the "do it themselves" small business owners. These dashboards allow the business owner to post once, and syndicate it to all the social media pages they choose and the content can hit their pages and audience of followers all at the same time. Each social media dashboard management has its own niche tool. A business owner needs to compare his or her functions against the goals to be achieved with social media marketing. At the top of the social media dashboard tools is Hootsuite, followed by Every Post, Social Oomph, Buffer, and Social Sprout. Depending on the sophistication of your business's social media campaign, some of these dashboard platforms may charge a fee.

Keeping track of an employee's productivity is also critical in projecting payroll cost, project management cost, staff allocation to a specific task or job, and measuring the success of employee job performance. Time Management tools are available to small businesses to increase productivity.

Businesses that depend on tracking time are most vulnerable to the loss of billable work hours without having an effective time management tool in place. Businesses that have these systems down to a science include attorney firms, consulting firms, and accounting firms. Other businesses that can benefit from the integration of a time management tool or system include service businesses like landscaping, plumbing or heating contractors, or other home construction or maintenance service business.

Systems like Toggle can help a business "scale out" productive tasks and projects from services and duties that may not help the business make money. The business can then make better, more profitable decisions about the best use of their time by sticking to the specialties offered to customers. The software system Freedom was designed to block employees from engaging in distracting activities unrelated to the business's core purpose; it even has the ability to "time keep" employees on products and compare them against imposed deadlines. Freedom will disable social media and filter out internet sites on computers during designated work hours, while providing reminders and posts to the employee of their list of daily responsibilities.

Nutcache was designed to allow an employee to work on multiple projects at one time, with projects posted in folders. As the folders were opened and closed, and projects (such as data entry or typing) were added to, Nutcache would then track the movements of the project, and compare that to a database of time and materials standards. Remember the Milk is a program that provides a series of alerts to employees of their daily tasks and expected time lines. The employee can check off tasks as they are completed, and will send a report to management.

A customer relationship management (CRM) tool will come in handy for the small business owner that conducts high volumes of sales spread among vast client audiences. The CRM has two basic functions. First, the CRM will help keep sales representatives on track within the sales process, so that sales representatives can properly fulfill the service of a sale with a client, including timelines, dates of requested delivery, payment tracking, and dribble marketing activities.

The other side of the CRM function for the small business owner is to monitor sales representative-client habit performance. Is the sales representative providing all the required details and information to the client? Why is the client only getting a personal visit or phone call once a month, when the demand shows the client needs further weekly engagement? Also, CRM systems can host all of the sales, marketing and advertising tools, order forms, and product information that a sales representative may need in order to better service the client's interest.

Many of these systems seem to overlap; however, they are designed with their own specific specialty, aimed at helping a small business to become better organized and profitable. They are designed to be integrated with other systems, so the small business can have an easy continuity of its operations, freeing up the business owner's time for other tasks, such as marketing and sales. Not every business needs to have all the systems mentioned. It is wise to get the advice of a seasoned business consultant and/or accountant when choosing the right systems for your small business enterprise.

eye candy
Yes, we're
OPEN

– CHAPTER 15 –
Hiring Your Weaknesses

Source: During most of their entrepreneurial journey, small business owners will wear many hats when managing and handling the numerous duties required to operate a small local business enterprise. How does the small business owner become profitable, freeing themselves from necessary tasks of day-to-day business, while not neglecting areas of their business? They must focus on hiring their weaknesses.

As a new business owner, it may seem that you will be wearing many hats. Before you have a workforce to rely on, you are an army of one, in charge of every task and duty involved in operating your small business enterprise. You must go to work to get the work so you can go to work to make a profit. Did you get all of that? Meaning: you're the first line of defense in marketing and selling your business, your story, your products and/or services, as well as yourself to potential customers.

Next, you are responsible for fulfilling the customer's request, and for collecting on the products sold or services rendered.

Meanwhile, you are also the one responsible for marketing and advertising; the one in charge of networking with potential clients in your community; and the one with the duties of stocking the shelves and maintaining a positive and clean, appearance to your store front.

At first it will seem overwhelming to handle all of these responsibilities. A new business owner must come to terms with what they can effectively handle, with each task done correctly, while achieving positive results for their business.

Each business owner must honestly discern their strengths and weaknesses. It is only through this very humbling experience that a business owner sets aside ego and becomes teachable and open to delegating tasks to other people.

So how does a business owner know what their best skill sets are? Start with a clean sheet of white paper, and make a list of all the reasons you started your business. Make another list of all the tasks and responsibilities you enjoy while operating your business. Then list all the tasks you don't enjoy (or find rewarding) within the day-to-day operations of the business, but yet are critical functions. Then think about this for a moment… are the tasks that you do not enjoy doing within your realm of skills?

Take time to rank each task on a scale of one through ten, with one being the score given to a task that you are least confident in doing or least educated or trained in, including tasks that you are not willing to become educated or trained in; this will help you in defining both your strongest skills and your weaknesses, giving you a baseline of which jobs to source out to an independent contractor or delegate to an employee.

So, what is the best use of the business owner's time? Usually it is the business owner who is the leading sales representative. Potential customers want to know the story and the message behind the scenes that makes the business stand out from others like it in the surrounding area.

It is the business owner, founder, that tells this story best, including why s/he decided to go down the self-employment track. The business owner needs to dedicate time to building relationships with multiple audiences. They will need to have positive relationships with other business owners, which sometimes become customers, with vendors and suppliers; with professionals (such as accountants or attorneys); with local community leaders; and with potential customers.

This will require the business owner to set aside time to network with these different groups of people. The business owner needs to spend time researching new product or service offerings, sometimes requiring the business owner to travel to trade shows or attend events that showcase the latest innovations. The business owner also is at the lead in providing customer service.

A business owner must look at financial metrics of the best use of their time. There are several methods for calculating where the business and business owner's time must be focused in order for the business to realize a profit.

My approach is looking at the bigger picture, then "reverse engineering" this model to put a plan in motion. The business owner should focus their best use of time on activities and goals that will enable them to arrive at their determined benchmarks. All other tasks that do not directly help achieve these goals can be delegated.

For instance, if your business requires an income of $125 per hour for every hour it is open to break even on its operating expenses, as well as providing the owner with profit, then the business owner needs to focus their activities on things that will contribute to the goal of generating income.

Tasks such as property maintenance or cleaning of the business or storefront should be delegated. It might cost the business owner a few hundred dollars a month to have their business maintained and cleaned by an outside service; however, it's the value of that time the business owner can now dedicate toward their goals that matters.

Tasks such as office or property maintenance, cleaning and stocking of store front shelves, or cleaning of tools, are all examples of minimum wage activities that take the business owner from core duties toward making the business more profitable. This is where a business owner can hire someone part-time to handle these jobs. This is considered a weakness for the business owner, because these tasks do not generate an income.

There are two methods by which a business owner can hire their weaknesses. The first method is hiring third parties to handle functions of their business, on a project by project basis, where these tasks do not require a full-time employee on site.

A business owner may opt to hire a bookkeeper, accountant, and/or payroll service that are given the responsibilities for maintaining records of the financial transactions of the business, the filing of taxes, and dealings with all the HR management aspects of the business's workforce. A business owner might decide to "farm out" their marketing and advertising to a branding and marketing company to handle the creation and development of the business's marketing collateral, ad placement, social media and digital marketing campaigns, as well as develop a website and other public awareness campaigns. A business owner may also choose to hire a landscaper or janitorial service to maintain the business's location or storefront.

The other method for hiring your weaknesses is to hire direct employees to work for your business. You may have a hair salon and be an expert hair stylist, but find it difficult to answer the phone and book appointments while trying to provide service to the client in front of you. If so, you can hire a receptionist that can handle and manage customer service over the phone. You might be experiencing growth and need additional people to help service your already successful flow of customers; you would be in search of employees that have similar skill sets to offer so they can assist in servicing your customers. Maybe your business is a retail business, and you need a stock clerk, in which that person can also be trained to be a cashier.

When hiring your weaknesses, whether you hire a third party that will handle a project or an employee, there are things to keep in mind. Not every employee or independent contractor will have the same passion about your vision or your business. Not every potential employee or contractor will share the same core values as you do. Not every employee will be as loyal to your business's mission as you expect. For some people, a job is just a job; a way for their needs to be met, and their expectation of responsibility and loyalty to the business ends when the employee clocks out at the end of their shift.

There are some practices that a small business owner can utilize in weeding out potential employees that may not be a good fit for their business. By establishing a set of standards and clearly communicating those standards, you are providing the potential employee a chance to continue to search for a more suitable employment environment closer to their own expectations.

During an interview a small business owner and potential employer can take additional steps to assure a good fit at their business. The potential employer can take the temperature of the scale of passion a potential employee may have about the business or industry. Ask the interviewee what they know about your business and the industry. You may also want to pose questions about the business to see if the potential employee did their homework.

You may ask the potential employee if they have any professional relationships with any of your other employees, vendors, clients, and/or independent contractors. If the person answers yes, you can ask how the potential employee developed these relationships. Ask if they have any other additional professional relationships or business contacts that they would offer up to the business as a potential employee, vendor, suppliers, clients, and/or contractors. Also, ask if they are a member of any local or regional trade organizations.

When explaining your small business and the potential employment opportunity, you need to be clear about the job task and duties, as well as the expectations of any required deadlines and benchmarks, making sure the potential employee completely understands the role for which they are applying. Showcase your business/company culture, providing a real-time view for the potential employee to see the business in live action. Also, share your business's core values and code of ethics, clearly communicating to the potential employee your standards of professional conduct.

If you are not sure about hiring the person long term, yet the potential employee has the skills you feel will help your business, you can offer to hire the person on a trial period. A trial period gives both the employer and the employee a way out if the relationship is not what either each party expected without any hard animosity. If the potential employee performs to the standards and expectations set forth in the initial interview, you can offer the option of full time long term employment to the new candidate. The potential employee also has the ability to hold open the doors of opportunity with other potential employers if the current employment situation is not a good fit.

You do not have to settle on the first potential employee that applies to your business. If your business is in dire need of the right person for the job, continue to operate until you have found the right person. Many small businesses struggle; they need people to get jobs done, and will hire someone hoping to find the relief they were looking for. It is your business, and if the applicant is not a good fit, then it is okay to be honest in telling them so.

In order to protect the interest of your small business, its vendors, clients, and other employees, you will want to vet the potential employee. You can require the candidate to take a drug test; via a third party that specializes in this service. You can require potential candidates to be subject to a background check, including looking at criminal history or military service. You can screen for unwanted behavior.

There are a host of employment questionnaires that you can obtain from a HR service that contain questions which would test the character of a potential employee by the way the potential employee's answers match the questions. You can ask them to write an essay on why they might be a good fit for your business and the value they bring to the table. You may check with the potential employee's references and former employers.

You cannot however ask personal questions related to the candidate's age, marital status, sexual orientation, religious affiliation, or race. There are both federal and state employment laws which protect potential employees from discrimination, or acts of employment discrimination based on personal disposition.

As a small business, you may not be in the best position financially to hire the highest qualified talent. Let's face reality - your buying power may be limited and you may not be able to afford to offer the same perks as major corporations. So, a small business must be creative in what it can offer potential employees.

Most small business operations do not have the capital to compete with corporate giants. They are not in a position to offer retirement packages, full health care benefits, or large financial compensation packages. So how does a small business attract, hire, and retain the right employees?

The business can offer other sets of benefits and perks that may be non-traditional in corporate settings. Some perks that could be offered include a flexible work schedule that is accommodating to both the business's hours of operation and the schedule of the potential employee. Small businesses can provide performance bonuses or incentives for employees when they assist in the growth of the business. A small business can allow for an employee to telecommute when applicable, saving the employee commuting costs.

A small business can offer to pay for additional education or training while on company time. Learn to earn programs have become very popular for small businesses. A business can promise to pay all or part of a tuition fee for higher learning or job training. The employee will agree to stay with the business for a term agreed upon by the business owner and the employee. Once the term has been fulfilled, the tuition is paid for, or reimbursed , to the employee by the business owner. If the employee leaves prematurely to the end of the agreed term, then the business owner would only have to cover a portion of the tuition, and the employee would be responsible for the rest. This helps the employee advance their career and the business to retain talent.

A small business can offer to compensate the employee with commute cost reimbursement. Some employees must travel up to two hours away to stay employed at their current situation. The small business can offer to assist with tolls and parking expenses, and offer the employee a fuel card with a pre-determined allowance. These are also valid tax deductions for a small business. A small business may allow for a small expense account for the employee, predetermined to cover cost of office supplies used at home when the employee is telecommuting. Other perks a small business may opt to offer are employee discounts on the business's products/services. Some small businesses do contribute to a retirement fund that the employee may take with them when the employee moves to another place of employment, if the employee met the term of their employment with the business.

Some businesses, in an attempt to retain employees, will offer ownership interest in the business to the employee. There is the rare occasion that an employee will invest as much time into the business as the small business owner does. The business owner may then choose to make the employee a partner in the business. The employee has the incentive to see the business become a success and commits to the business long term.

So, where do you go to hire your weaknesses? Today there are a plethora of options. Websites and social media sites like LinkedIn, Monstor.com, Craig's List, and Meet Up are prime places to post employment ads and allow for two-way engagement between a potential employee and business owner. Also, you can utilize the services of an employment agency or head hunting firm. These types of firms already have a data base of potential candidates that may fit the criteria of someone you desire to fulfill a job role.

A small business can offer a mentorship or apprenticeship opportunity to business students in high school and/

or college. These students are in search of employment experience as part of their coursework. If the student proves to be a success during the term of the apprenticeship, you can offer the student part- or full-time employment. Also, you can ask for referrals from your current employees. Employment One Stop Labor Centers may also offer candidates that are currently receiving unemployment benefits and in search of a job.

Whatever the type of employment arrangement, as a small business owner, you must be able to delegate the tasks that occupy your time and take you away from income-producing activities; be willing to let go of a little control. No employee will ever know all the things you know. No employee will ever do things in the exact manner that you would do things. When you are hiring your weaknesses, you must have a level of trust in the professionals you are hiring; make them feel comfortable in helping your business solve problems, and give them the latitude to do so.

Section IV:
Completing the Marketing Package

eye candy
Yes, we're
OPEN

– CHAPTER 16 –

Branding the Right Message for Your Business

Source: A company's brand is more than just a logo or graphic; it is the internal and external message a business represents to its employees, investors, clients, and to the surrounding community. It is one which best describes what that business does, why it exists, as well as what the business and its leadership believes in. What does your brand say about your company? What should be considered when branding your business?

So you just founded your venture. It could be a local, small, family owned Main Street business or a large endeavor with hopes to expand globally, creating a far reaching effect.

Regardless of the size of your business, the message you choose to send to "the street" is paramount in explaining what type of business you have; the purpose your business serves; the product or service it offers; and the demographic populace and geographic locale in which you offer your value creation.

The next step many people do is go about getting a logo or graphic created so they have an image to place on their business card. Then, when they pitch their business, there is a visual reminder about their company. Initially, this can be a costly mistake for many business owners.

It is important for a business owner to have an understanding of the entire meaning behind "branding" a company; this should include the completion of a branding exercise, crucial for that company's foundational success. As a business out- grows their initial logo or changes its product/ service offering mix, the logo becomes obsolete.

Branding is more than just a logo or a font. It is the representation of all the internal and external factors about the company, translated into a set of graphics and text that tell the "elevator pitch" about the company; reminding people about all the dimensions of that business.

Branding exercises and creation by a full-service marketing and advertising firm can cost thousands of dollars, but the investment in the long run can save tens of thousands, hundreds of thousands, or even millions in having to re-brand a business owner's company and/or lost business due to the wrong message sent about the company to potential customers.

There are many factors that should be taken into consideration when learning how to properly brand one's company. As founders of a business or an entrepreneurial enterprise, sometimes personal preferences get in the way of selecting company logo or graphic color schemes. Instead, it should be the story that tells the "why" behind the business that should be the deciding factor of the imagery and content selected for sharing a company's message with the public.

Just because the entrepreneur thinks it's a cool look does not mean that the general public will understand the logo, or even be able to identify with its significance. That is why much thought, attention, and detail must be taken when deciding the final translation of a company brand.

The message you send to potential audiences about your company needs to be with a definite purpose in mind. It should summarize, in brief, the products and services being provided, and why the products and services should be deemed noteworthy by potential customers.

Behind every business is a leader, or a group of leaders that are the drivers of that business; the "why" they embrace, should be reflected throughout the context of the brand. Your brand should also have consistency throughout the entire purpose, or scope, of the company. Nothing is more confusing to a potential customer than picking some logo or tag saying that fails to reflect all of the company's products/services.

When branding a company, consider internal factors equally with the external message desired to be shared with clients. Internal branding is a reflection of a company's internal core values, including a code of ethics, morals and beliefs, how the company should be organized, and the disciplines within the company an owner desires their staff to adopt.

Internal branding should examine any message the employees need to understand. Using words such as "the company," or "this business" versus, "the team," and "our associates," creates very distinct feels. A business owner should want to create a work experience where their employees realize they are part of a greater cause, and their contributions are part of the greater success of the company, not one that fosters a culture of "cut throat - every person for themselves" job environment.

Words and phrases such as previously mentioned, are located in a company employee handbook, on the company website, or on social media. How social media marketing is utilized will reflect the internal culture of any company.

Language selection is extremely important. It is so powerful and can either be very inviting and attractive to the right individuals, or it can be a total turn off for some. Oftentimes, businesses focus on the external message they desire to purport without considering long term branding strategies for expanding their business, which would include recruiting talent to assist with such growth.

It is important to understand that an external message is more than just a sales pitch. The most valuable brands in the world don't sell products, but the brand itself, for it has been said, "People don't buy products, they buy brands."

That means that a company's brand must contain more information than just the products and/or services being sold.

Within the external brand, its' symbolism (which is the logo, color scheme, and anything visual) as well as the content (tag lines, by-lines, copy in ads, and anything auditory) should say what the business believes in and stands for; product/service offered; and the audience it serves without saying it. That may sound confusing, but this is the most complicated consideration when choosing all the moving parts in successfully branding a business to the public.

Most marketing and advertising firms will usually begin the branding journey with a series of discovery sessions in order to gain a better understanding of the founders/leadership of the business.

Part of the exercise is finding out the "why" behind the decision to go into business in the first place; to discover the purpose that has driven someone to take their invention or creation to the next level.

Personality and core values are taken into consideration when trying to include a story being portrayed to the public. This is part of "why" the potential customer should purchase a company's product or service.

Next, the branding expert will want information regarding all of the moving parts of an owner's business. This will include a company's current status, as well as what the company is expected to look like in five, ten, and even twenty-five years from now. The bigger picture is reflected as part of the brand.

Branding experts will take a deep look at which target audience is the right fit for your company's product or service. They will research the demographic and geographic of every potential target client, and align them with what you have to offer. To many business owner's and entrepreneur's surprise, the target market they intended to sell to may not be the right or best fit, after the branding research demonstrates larger opportunities, not originally considered.

Maybe a product or service is better suited for sales opportunities overseas where there is a greater need for a company's invention. It is also possible that research may show an initial targeted audience to be lesser in volume of numbers than originally considered, but may be willing to pay more per individual sale for the item planning to be marketed. The branding exercises reveal many options and truths about a business that an owner may have never realized.

Branding experts add value to a company because their train of thought is objective and concise. They examine a business, its products and services, as well as the owner's positioning without judgement or bias. Branding experts are not working on behalf of any client nor are they working on the owner's behalf (as in the founder, whom usually has an emotional tie to their value creation and company).

These experts take a pragmatic approach to review all aspects of a business, utilizing logic, statistics and research, and understanding on how the company's potential audience should respond to the brand that ultimately translates the business's message. They do this through a systematic series of questions and exercises. The more detail and time that is spent on the initial branding exercises, the more precise the branding expert will be in coining the logo, tag line, and content about the business.

A branding expert should be a company's marketing department's best friend, one that remains available throughout all phases of a company's growth. Having the ability to work with one branding expert will assist you in the expediency to re-brand your company, for the initial branding expert already knows your back story and has monitored your growth.

A changing message, product/service line expansion, or the retelling of a story are all taken into consideration. The expert can eventually envision the business's journey much the same as the company's leadership, which will allow for consistent brand continuity throughout the entire company's life cycle.

It would be foolish to think that small local businesses only need a logo. Investing in appropriately telling the company's story to the public will have a direct result on the public developing a belief as to why they should patron a particular business.

Today, it is critical that small local businesses invest into proper branding as much as a major corporation, If it is to outlast the competition, as well as remain intriguing enough to the average consumer considering to give your business a try, this branding is essential. A company's brand should be strong enough to reflect all of its internal and external messages while providing a need to be part of the "cult following" of the brand a company represents.

A brand should carry a sense of value and integrity. Consumers don't trust products or sales people; they trust brands - brands that follow through on their word even when everything is not perfect. The most profitable of companies in the world understand that their brand is more than a brand; it's a culture and practice that consumers have come to trust, making good on its promises, even when it made a mistake. This takes patience, for great brands are built over time.

Branding is an investment in your self, your company, your value creation, your value proposition, and the statement you desire to make in the marketplace. The right brand will last a life time, while others will fade away. So brand wisely.

– CHAPTER 17 –

Essential Must Have Marketing Tools For Your Small Business

Source: Quick to gain a cult consumer following and loyal customer base, most businesses begin to advertise their product and/or service offerings without a plan. This can cause the business to spend valuable dollars in advertising which may not be the right fit in attracting potential clients from specific targeted audiences. In order to reach any group of potential customers effectively, every small business needs essential marketing tools that will help them better use their advertising budgets toward reaching more clients for potential deal acquisition.

A quality marketing plan, which includes an advertising campaign and an ongoing on-line presence, is the best place for a small business to invest their financial focus. Yet most small business owners say they cannot afford it.

I tell them that they cannot afford to be invisible and allow their competition to gain all the potential customers. A small business can invest tens of thousands or even hundreds of thousands of dollars on advertising and see absolutely no results. The reasons: in order to know what types of advertising will best suit your business reach, you need to understand your goals and targets, your ideal clientele, and posess a defined, available budget for marketing and advertising.

With the plethora of choices, where do you begin? It can be a daunting task and it can be easy to get overwhelmed; however, there are some tools that every small business must have to keep them on point and remain actively focused on their goals.

A business needs a quality marketing campaign. Notice I said, "quality". There are folks out there that will charge you thousands of dollars on a marketing plan, without taking the time to understand your business.

The most complete marketing exercise involves an outside marketing and branding firm taking the time to research your business goals, your personal goals as the business owner, your vision, and your core values. They then take all of this data and compile it into a report that is the foundation for the road map for the most ideal client acquisition for your business. The marketing plan aligns your value proposition product or service with the ideal demographic of potential client within a geographic territory.

In order to stay in front of people, you need a quality advertising plan that properly represents your message to the public. Again, I mention the word "quality." Any sales representative can give you an ad buy kit with the list of prices for ad space in the newspaper or on radio.

However, a quality advertising campaign is going to take into account all of the audience you specifically want to reach (based on demographics and geographic region), and provide you multiple avenues with which to gain an audience with these potential clients. Your advertising campaign should be a mix of traditional advertising and online campaigns, with a detail of expected reaches.

Advertising results should be measurable, so that new client acquisition ratio can be properly assessed. This would look like, "x number of advertising dollars spent = x number of new clients," and then, broken down dollar for dollar, with the return on the investment into advertising. Utilizing this plan will allow you to gauge the most effective advertising medias for your business.

Living in a digital era, you must be able to have an effective website that is mobile friendly. Your website is your business card to the world. As technology continues to evolve, so should your website's abilities to be searched for and found on multiple types of devices. About 80% of individuals under the age of 40 use their mobile device for email, internet searches, and financial transactions. If your website is not mobile friendly, then your business will not be seen. Your website should also be able to support video, audio, and have multiple placements for a call to action, that excite the viewer and engage them into wanting to know more or make a purchase.

Keep an open mind to alternative forms of payment. Paper money, coins, and debit/credit cards are just a few ways people pay for things today. You need to expand your horizon to be able to accept crypto-currency, electronic wallet payments, and/or barter. Once you have decided on which platforms of payment your business will accept, you need to include it in your advertising materials. There are folks who are loyal to one payment preference over another, and you need to let them know you are in a position to service their needs.

Cause marketing must be a part of our overall marketing strategies if you are going to have community brand value. Younger consumers do take notice of businesses that donate to local community causes and charities. They will patron those businesses that offer back something to a non-profit cause, especially when it is a cause that the consumer can identify with. Your plan on giving back should be consistent year to year. A business can build out an event around their contribution to the good cause, which gets noticed by local media.

Have an alliance with a freelance news reporter associated with local media. With the consolidation of newspapers and media outlets across America, most news stories, articles, and press releases do not get published unless someone with press credentials submits them to the reporting news wires.

Most newspapers and publications have cut their staff and pluck from the news wires to save money on hiring dedicated reporters, as well as the time required for getting content ready for print. Most freelance news reporters, journalists, and/or investigative reporters have credentials to submit content to news wires. When a reporter or journalist submits the content, it is deemed more credible since the reporter has to vet the facts.

Hard physical marketing takeaways are still relevant, especially when you are marketing your business at a trade show or at a special buying market event. Business cards are still the number one marketing tool when you are making an introduction to another party for the first time. Many folks fail to carry a business card on their person. Other marketing materials such as brochures, sell sheets, and post card mailers, are take away items that a client will have in their hand as a reminder to consider making a purchase. Letter head and thank you cards are also a must.

Branding your business is more than selecting a clip art logo. There are many generic logo designs to choose from in clip art or online. Today, the attention span of a consumer is less than 15 seconds, and if your logo is not dynamic enough, you will fall into the trap of getting lost in the sauce. Your logo should be the beacon of your brand, the message you wish to share, and the explanation of what you do without a lengthy conversation.

You can take the time and make the investment to have the right logo crafted that will last for decades or you can waste time and money on getting a generic logo design. In the end, if you choose the latter, you will also create channel confusion with your customer audience because they may stumble through in the transition from one branding to the next.

Large numbers of sales may not be generated from engagement about your product or service is now mandatory in a world where good news is noticed, but bad press moves at lightning speed. Social media business pages should not just be a bull horn for shouting to potential audiences to purchase your goods/services; it should be a platform of education.

Consider including in your business's social media campaign, content in which your business provides informative, engaging material and interesting facts to folks about your field of practice that potential consumers may not otherwise be aware of. Social media business pages on Facebook, LinkedIn, and others are not the place to tell your business's story, but to provide snippets of information which will peak the potential client's interest. A small introductory video about your business is an extra step that assures you someone will take notice of your business.

You Tube is the premier platform for hosting video content in marketing your product and/or service, regardless of how big or small your company may be. The best part is that it is a free service for you to use, and the step-by-step upload process gives your video additional search engine optimization so your video will rank higher in more relevant searches. Over time you can add to your video library content that can be re-purposed and shared in social media campaigns, or videos that can be sent to potential clients as part of your dribble marketing practices.

It is suggested the shorter the introductory video, the better. This takes some practice in trying to fit in who you are, what your business does, where you are located, what your value proposition is, why you are better than your competitor, and what's in it for the viewer of the video - all in less than 30 seconds.

Search engine ranking has become more and more competitive as the race to capture command over key words and ad word phrases intensifies on the internet. You will need a SEO plan that is phased in over time and that will stay relevant as your business expands in products and/or services offered. This will take careful consideration as you prepare a set of words and phrases that are unique to your business and industry situation, while being relevant to the common consumer. This is so that your business shows up on their radar, preferably on the first or second pages of their internet search.

The more upfront time, resources, and thought you invest into your business's marketing tools, the more productive your results will be in staying in front of potential clients and while retaining top of the mind awareness with your current clients.

eye candy
857
Yes, we're
OPEN

– CHAPTER 18 –

Online Marketing Tools for Small Businesses

Source: In today's multi-media and digital marketing world, small business owners have multiple choices of low- or no-cost options for promoting their business, in addition to traditional marketing and advertising tools and practices designed to aid the local business in becoming noticed by potential consumers.

Traditionally, before the internet and mobile devices, marketing and advertising options were limited and costly for the small business owner. Most small business owners would look to advertising in the newspaper, on local television or radio, or even handouts and flyers placed on car windshields and in mailboxes. As technology advanced, so did all the methods to stay out in front of your competitors and customers. There are several tools online to help a locally owned business promote one's self which carries little or no cost.

At one time, the standard form of advertisement for a business was to be listed in the Yellow Pages, which was the business-commercial section of the phone book directory. However, times have changed with consumers relying mainly upon their mobile devices to communicate, and in some cases, not even having a home land line supported phone. In place of the Yellow Pages are websites and business directories such as Manta, Merchant Circle, and Tap Into.

Manta is a website which lists profiles of local businesses, and allows for consumers to leave a review after their experience of either purchasing a product or service. Manta allows for a business to set up a profile, including spotlighting the services and products a business has to offer. The profile serves as a business card to the digital world.

Manta also allows for local ranking of your business based on customer reviews and special awards a business may receive. Manta also has tools which allow local businesses to find other resources, and to connect with other small businesses to fulfill operational or vendor needs, all this without having to flip through pages of the phone book.

Businesses will benefit from using Manta. A small business can separate itself from the crowd of other similar local businesses by having customer reviews. New potential customers can use these as a point of reference in making a buying decision. When new potential clients see a number of positive reviews about a business, they also see local brand loyalty. Repeat customers tell a very different story to the market than having hundreds of one time customers.

Manta's ability for a business owner to see customer feedback and reviews will also allow for a business to identify areas in need of improvement within its business model.

Merchant Circle is another online business listing site. Merchant Circle is a platform that allows the locally owned business to connect and network with other locally owned businesses, sharing contacts and ideas, while helping to connect the business with potential customers. Merchant Circle had advanced their capabilities beyond just being a local business directory. Merchant Circle has combined the concepts of a local business directory and profiles with the tools of social media and marketing. Businesses can level up and purchase additional marketing services from Merchant Circle, focusing efforts on a specific geographic area.

Local online new sites, such as TAP Into, also offer free business listing directories. TAP Into focuses its hyper-local content in the State of New Jersey and surrounding areas, and is supported by the local business community. Local businesses can list their business contact and location information. Also, businesses can submit press releases to the local editors and publishers, giving businesses the ability to promote an announcement or event.

These sites can help a business in establishing an online content footprint. Businesses that have multiple articles, or key search words or phrases in their business profile description, are more likely to rank higher in search engines due to the amount of content. With so many people on the go relying on information at their fingertips from their mobile devices, if your business is not at least showing up on the first two or three pages of search engines, then your business will not be seen by new potential customers. Business listings with Manta, Merchant Circle, and local sites like TAP Into drastically change your local small business's placement within the rankings of search engines. I have even seen businesses that don't have their own website rank high in search engines because their business profiles are enhanced and provide a lot of detail to potential consumers.

Social media is the place a business should turn to in promoting their business wares and reaching new potential customers. Take your pick, there are many to choose from; however, the front runners for two-way engagement still stand with Facebook leading the way, followed by LinkedIn, Google Plus, Flickr, Tumblr, Twitter, and Instagram. Each social media platform offers something different and serves a specific purpose.

Facebook offers multiple tools for a small business. In addition to having your own personal profile page, which you may share content about your business to your friends, family, and connections, you can set up a separate page for your business.

Your Facebook business profile can double for both social media and as a bridge online until your business is able to pay for a professional website to be developed. Your Facebook business profile can be the first front in promoting your business's products or services online. There are several methods on how to put Facebook to work for your business. However, Facebook changes its algorithm to bury organic growth in the hopes that you would pay for advertising in order to reach new customers via the social media giant.

A good social media practice, which works well for promoting your business on Facebook, is to post content consistently. Either chose to post weekly, every few days, or every day, but be consistent in your posting habits. If you have something to promote about your business, post it to your business page first, then share it on your profile page from your business page. From your profile page, you can share the post to groups or to your friend's pages. This is one of the better ways to increase reaches of the post, so it all originates from your business page.

You will also want to diversify your content. What I have found that works best is posting a relevant article about a specific business industry related to my business, followed by a post spotlighting a product or service I offer the next day; then post a photo or video the following day, posting another product promotion or coupon, followed by another relevant article, and so on. Mixing up your content to include content originated by you and your business, and including interesting articles or videos originated by third parties, will help throw off Facebook's algorithm, and your post will have a higher probability of being viewed.

For the small business looking to spend a few dollars on advertising, the most effective form of advertising on Facebook has been boosting a post. These posts stand out above the daily post, and should focus on highlighting and increasing your reach to additional audiences. If you are trying to promote a business event or have an announcement or news that you feel will help generate additional foot traffic to your business's door, then boosting that post may be of great benefit. Make sure the boosted post has an eye-catching photo or video that will grab the attention of potential consumers immediately.

If your business has a specific product offering or brand, you may consider having a page dedicated to promoting the product brand aside from the company business page. The more places potential consumers see your product branding, the more likely they will want to try your product or service. Keep in mind, you should mix up the content between these pages. If your content on both your business page and product page is identical, Facebook may lower both pages ability to be seen. The key is to post different content to each page and you can tag the other page in the post.

LinkedIn offers both the business owner and the business a way to connect with professionals. I have found LinkedIn is not necessarily the place to sell products directly to an end user, unless your business model is business to business; however, if your business model is business to consumer, then LinkedIn will offer your business other benefits. LinkedIn can serve as a place to recruit future employees; one where profiles of professionals list their skill sets, education, industry accolades, and other important information to potential employers to see if the professional might be a good fit for your business.

Your business can also syndicate and post articles of interest on LinkedIn, which are spread throughout the news thread of your contacts. These informative articles, written by either you and/or one of your staff, will help you and your business to be coined as a "local industry expert," or an authority the professional audience can come to know and trust. Your business page on LinkedIn works like a consolidated version of your business's website, much like a business profile you would post to Manta or Merchant Circle. Because LinkedIn is reviewed as an authorized website, your business content posted to LinkedIn will sometimes rank higher on the search engines than your own business website.

Google Plus offers additional social media benefits for the small locally owned business and mixes a series of Google web services rolled into one platform. Google Plus is a place on which a business can create a profile, join networks, recommend other local locations, load up and share pictures and video, as well as offer a map with directions to the business's location. A business can integrate its web traffic analytical data with insights monitoring as part of its Google Plus page. Google has also acquired Zagat, which was a website service that allowed for customers to rate and rank businesses based on their customer experiences and reviews. This means a local business can also integrate the data from Zagat to enhance their overall web presence. Google Plus is free to use.

Twitter serves businesses to remind customers or alert new customers of current events, announcements, or deals. Twitter is a great way to catch the attention of a specific following and then redirect the audience to the action step you desire them to take. Twitter messages are limited to just 140 characters. Basically, Twitter is the text message platform of the internet. The best way a business can use Twitter is to announce specials and deals in real time. Twitter allows for a business to build an unlimited number of followers, thus giving businesses access to a wide spectrum of audience of potential customers.

They say a photograph is worth a thousand words. Platforms like Flickr, Tumblr, and Instagram have specialized in providing a photo journal online to be shared with family, friends, fellow colleagues, and potential customers. These platforms are designed to allow users to load up photographs in the moment and share them with their fan base instantaneously, in hopes of creating a real time feeling of "I wish I was there", for the person viewing the picture. This emotional trigger also can work well in creating a product demand in the moment. A business can feature a picture of a spotlighted product and offer a discount on their next purchase with the merchant to the first hundred people who comment.

What makes Instagram so popular is that it is shared across the social media platform Facebook. Flickr and Tumblr were acquired by Yahoo. These two platforms offer slightly different vantage points. Flickr allows for the upload and sharing of photos and video while Tumblr allows for video and content in short form, much like a mini-blog. All three of these platforms are free to use and are another way to establish a presence online for businesses that have small advertising budgets.

Video content ranks the highest on the internet. Video content is also the most sought after content in the leading search engines. Every smart phone or mobile device is now equipped to film short video. Small businesses can create their own small videos and post them to various video hosting platforms that will help a business establish a wider internet presence. The most popular of video social media sites is You Tube.

When posting to YouTube, make sure you include many of the search terms or key words that may relate to your business and the video you are posting. Even your title should be unique but yet searchable to your business. I discovered that having my business possesses its own You Tube Channel is very helpful. You can mix the video content to keep subscribers engaged. My video mix includes raw, behind-the-scenes footage, professionally filmed and edited commercials, recorded interviews and spotlights by mainstream and local news media, and I have even recorded a personal message and posted it to clients.

You can create a video on just about anything, from promoting an event or making a public announcement about your business, to sharing valuable information on subject matter or field practice related to your business. You can even show your clients and audience a how-to video. All these videos are content you can share as part of your social media campaign production. You can also place links on your social media and business website of videos that you want your customers to see when searching for information that might influence their buying decision.

Daily Motion is another video sharing platform that allows for the creation of user sharing groups and for videos to be recommended to other audiences. Vimeo, another video sharing platform, was the first of all the video platforms to offer high definition video capabilities. Vimeo's platform was developed to specialize in editing, hosting, and streaming video from mobile devices. Daily Motion, Vimeo, or You Tube can be used by your business. Be aware that some cross-video promotion is not accepted by the three platforms. Even Facebook now allows for video to be loaded on a business page.

Videos created with the purpose of capturing the attention of a new potential customer needs to grab the attention of the viewer within the first 15 to 30 seconds, or you will lose the attention of the viewer. Your video content should also be unique and have a different hook. There are tens of millions of videos posted between YouTube, Vimeo, and Daily Motion, so you will need to be creative in order for your video to be searchable and stand out among the crowd.

If your business is affiliated with a cooperative warehouse or parent distributor, there is a high likelihood that they also have a master website that offers marketing and advertising support. If you own a hardware store or auto parts store, such as a Hardware Hank or NAPA within your own store portal, these co-op groups will offer up a series of training and tools which are part of the support offered when you agree to promote their brand and purchase product from their distribution centers.

If your business does not have a website yet, you need to get one. You can acquire a domain name from Go Daddy, for just a few bucks a year. Create it yourself website platforms such as Wix, Word Press, and Web.com, provide several pre-existing templates. The most important pages to have for a very basic website include: a home page or landing page which is the first introduction to visitors about your business and its products/services; a contact us page, which includes the hours of operation, information about your products and/or services, as well as a list of the most popular or unique products/services you provide; and lastly, the about us page, giving visitors a little more information about the business and you as the owner.

Monthly e-newsletters are another way to stay in front of your customers. Email newsletters should not be a large book or difficult to read. It should inform the reader of two or three key areas about your business. Maybe you're going to have a product or service sale or host a special event; email newsletters are a great way to keep your customers reminded of your business events, promotions and updates. You can also offer up an informative article (about 200 to 400 words) that will help educate your audience on how to make a better buying decision or create public awareness about a cause your business supports. The online tools and services of Mail Chimp or Constant Contact offer a variety of low cost options to reach your current clients.

It may seem overwhelming at first, that, on top of all your other business responsibilities, you now must spend time in front of your computer marketing your business, and, yes, there are many options to employ. There are tools to help you manage your online efforts. Two tools that will help you measure and manage your online presence are Google Analytics and Hoot Suite. Google Analytics can help you measure your marketing ranking and efforts online, so you can eliminate less effective online marketing. Google Analytics will also give you essential data to enhance the online marketing that is helping create customer flow for your business. Hoot Suite is a digital dashboard that you can use for managing and posting content to multiple social media sites at one time, thus saving you time having to make daily posts to each individual site.

The choice is yours. You can choose to spread your

marketing efforts over multiple, digital platforms or you can choose to stick to one or two tools. Local businesses that employ multiple online channels to promote their business are usually the businesses that have the most physical foot traffic in their door. Once they are in the door it's up to you to provide the best experience to keep them coming back and tell their friends and neighbors about you and your business.

eye candy
857
Yes, we're
OPEN

– CHAPTER 19 –

Content is King

Source: Any business looking for a mechanism by which to gain a competitive edge in getting in front of new potential customer must have an understanding between quality and quantity of marketing content; content does matter.

Marketing is changing all the time, and so is the variety of content that is spread throughout the internet, mobile devices, and other forms of media. Small businesses must consider taking a new perspective; time and money spent on marketing is a necessary evil, and should be reviewed as an investment instead of a cost. Traditionally small businesses would purchase full page ads in local newspapers and publications.

There has been a migration from traditional print to digital media. When potential consumers search the web for information about a small business, they will find a menu of information, i.e., reviews, websites, news articles, and social media posts. If you want to command what potential consumers see, then you must take command of the content that is being posted about your business. You must be the king of your online content.

Whether you focus your efforts on authoring written content, creating videos, recording audios, or posting on social media, your business needs to post new content on a consistent basis. Whether you choose to post content monthly, weekly, or daily, there must be consistency in the frequency of your content strategy. Not only consistency, but the strength of your content matters as well.

A key strategy to keep in mind when authoring content is to make sure your content includes key words and phrases to show up in the top of a search engine as the most relevant key words. You will need to research the key words and phrases that relate to your business and industry; sprinkle these terms into your content, and maximize your content's ability to be searched and show up on the first few pages of a search engine. Whenever posting a video or photo, it's important to take advantage of search engine optimization tools so that your video or business photo also ranks higher.

The practice and process of search engine optimization will allow for any form of content to rank higher, resulting in a higher probability of the content being seen. I would suggest taking part in a brain storm exercise. Write down on a piece of paper a list of terms, words, and phrases that best describe the nature of your business, what your business offers, and the industry segment your business represents. Choose the top twenty terms that fit your business the best. Make sure to have a few terms or phrases that are of local relevance, meaning if you own an auto parts store in Pine Bush, New York, you will want one of your key words or phrases to be "Auto Parts Pine Bush New York."

There are several types of content that are offered in promoting your business. There are authored forms of content which include press releases, articles, web blogs, e-books, online business profiles, and even the content on your business's website. A business benefits from having a healthy mix of authored content. Knowing how to author the content will assist you in your overall strategy.

Press releases are a powerful tool to inform potential consumers about your business. Your business might be launching a new product, celebrating an event, or maybe your business partnered up with a recognized brand in the market place; press releases are effective in obtaining air time for your business without the high cost of advertising. Press releases can be posted to a website for media to scrub and report on your local business event. You can employ the services of a new wire such as PR Web or 24/7 Press Release; which will syndicate your press release to the many media outlets that utilize these news wires for content in serving their audience. A press release can also be sent to your local news outlet, either newspaper or public access television channel or local radio.

An effective press release with a catchy headline will lure the attention of potential consumers. Press releases that capture the eye of a news reporter will always be the headline that jumps off the page. Within the first paragraph, state your case to the reader. In most cases, you have only fifteen to thirty seconds to gain the attention of a reader. The most critical information should be prioritized in the first paragraph. Include supportive facts. If it's numbers, provide a summary of the data; if it's an event, the dates and times matter.

Your press release should be flawless. Grammar mistakes are signs of a hack and new publications will not syndicate content that is deemed not credible. Insight provided by you, the owner of the business, as well as some words from a client, will help lend further credibility to your press release. Quotes and captions not only enhance the article, they invite the reader to be a part of the discussion. You will want to include a call to action, contact information where a reporter can reach you, and a reference point to conduct additional research.

Articles are expanded perspectives covering a specific subject matter related to your business. Generally, they should be reserved as public awareness and educational tools that a potential consumer can review, aiding in making better buying decisions. Articles should not be a sales pitch. They assist the local business owner in becoming an authority within their industry and market segment. Articles can be altered for publication in a web blog or an article post on LinkedIn, or even on a business's website.

As you create more articles, you can offer your content to various publications to syndicate the content. Local newspapers, regional magazines, and trade briefs are always in search of content that they do not have to purchase. This lends an advantage to your business by getting your name in front of potential consumers and throughout the community as a branded expert. These articles become an indirect sell in establishing a relationship with the reader. When they see you behind the counter of your local business, there could be a new-found trust in you, which the reader and potential customer then translates as trust of financial transactions with your business.

Web blogging can be a very effective way of creating online content for you and your business. Blogging creates awareness to potential consumers that your business exists. Blogging provides an opportunity for search engines to rank your website and business higher, due to the incorporation of key words and phrases within the blog post itself. Blog posts can be syndicated and shared on a business's social media pages, thus furthering the reach of content seen by others. Blog posts can also offer additional information to a potential consumer about your product or service, which may not be reflected or spoken about on a product's packaging or in a formal piece of advertising. Think of blog post as additional discovery for the potential consumer enabling them to make an educated buying decision. Blog posts that get many views become blog posts that command authority.

In authoring an article or blog post, keep your audience in mind. Integrate language and terms that the audience will respect and view as educated and of value. Much like a press release, a blog post needs a catchy headline that will jolt the potential reader to take a closer look at the content.

Be mindful of the purpose of the blog post or article. Is it to educate the potential consumer about an issue that plagues your industry? Are you trying to provide guidance on how to do something? Stick to the purpose and core subject matter. Reserve other runaway thoughts for additional blog post ideas.

Whereas a press release may contain four hundred to eight hundred words, a blog post or article can be a bit lengthier; from one thousand to fifteen hundred words. And just the same as an article, your blog post should include a call to action, whether it asks the reader to visit a website or sign up for a free gift. Once you have educated the reader and have their attention, you will want them to take action.

E-books are longer versions of articles, made available in a PDF version for potential consumers in search of more information. Since e-books can be hosted on your business's website, they are a valuable way to employ a maximum amount of content with a high frequency of key words and phrases, while still offering valuable information to the audience. Within the e-book you can tell a story and provide information, while pointing to pedigree examples of lessons learned and applied in your own life, habits and business.

Not all content is written. Photos and video content ranks the highest on search engines. Video is the most sought after content, so if you do not yet have any video content about your business, it's time to put video into high gear. A mix of video content is highly suggested. Applied to hypothetical business situations, if you were an owner of a lumber yard or home improvement store, you could roll out a video series on how to conduct home improvements in a step by step process. Within each segment you can explain the materials you used and where to find them. Video content aimed at gaining the attention of a consumer can double for advertising materials and social media post. These videos should be no longer than thirty to sixty seconds.

Setting up a YouTube Channel where, on a consistent basis you upload new video content, will help in making your You Tube Channel more relevant. Other video platforms mentioned previously, such as Vimeo and Daily Motion, give your business more online content power. Your content needs to be creative and unique. It is helpful for your personality and your business's culture to shine through to the audience; it's what will distinguish your business from other like businesses selling similar products.

With video, you can offer a schedule of rolling content to potential consumers to emphasize urgency. Videos posted about sales of specific product brands and the duration of the sale will entice consumers to act now. You can set up an interview style video where one of your employees explains the importance of the business's existence within the community. Most phones and digital cameras are very capable of filming quality video for placement online; these types of videos only need to be a few minutes long. Video costs almost nothing to create; the advantage of video is the low cost of self-produced and posted content.

Photographs have a way to send a message without saying a word. Photographs of people in captured moments, whether it be in motion during a work task, or staff pictured at a non-profit event, or even pictures of products within a store, can all be used to tell a story. Pictures of the "product of the week" or "featured sale of the week" not only make for additional blog content, they double as content for social media posts. The most popular of photograph-sharing social media platforms is Instagram. A business can choose to use Tumblr or Flickr depending on the need to host photographs online. Even your captions and headlines of photographs are a place for you to strengthen your search engine optimization by using key words to describe the photos.

For your content to be king over your competitors, you will need to consider a number of concepts when authoring and posting written content, photos, or videos, allowing your content to stand out. Unique and original content is most remembered by potential consumers. There could be fifty articles that share how to save money when shopping;

however, there might be only ten articles that share how to save money when shopping for deals at a hardware store. Getting specific will direct your efforts in crafting original and unique articles and blog posts. Eye catching, emotional headlines entice readers to investigate further by actually reading your article or blog.

Your content, whether written, photo, audio or video, should be something a potential consumer can immediately apply to their own situation. If the content provided has an actionable influence, that content is more valuable to the reader. Offer tools to the reader so that they are more tempted to take action and can measure the effectiveness of the content's value as applied to their own situation.

Content should solve a problem. People usually search for information when they are trying to solve a problem, even if it is to learn how to do something. A reader will try to learn how to do something because they must take on a task they do not yet know how to address. Content should either aim to solve a problem or provide additional information on how to solve the reader's current challenge.

If you are citing works or research, be certain of the accuracy of the source of data or research referenced in your articles, blogs, and e-books. Where you obtain your data, and how you recognize it, not only shows your integrity (that you give credit where credit is due), but also the source is a recognized authority. You never want to use a piece of research that you come to find out is false or misleading;

it will only diminish your expert credibility to potential consumers and online readers.

Engaging your audience in the discussion means to get them excited about the content you have provided, and to influence them to take a position. The entire reason for authoring or producing content is to educate readers on specific subject matter so they make a buying decision, hopefully one that is in favor of your business. Content should strike a chord with the reader and potential consumer that makes them want to spur into action. Sometimes the addition of video or photographs can enhance the message you wish to convey.

You will want to get into a consistent rhythm in providing content to your new readership following. After a while, readers will automatically expect updated content from you, so you need to think about how you will pace yourself so you don't run short of ideas or content. Most small businesses post an article or new content to a blog once a month. Consider a similar strategy for your photo and video content campaigns.

Lastly, if you desire to be the king of your content, speak or write from a place of personal experience. Potential consumers and readers always want to know that the creator of the content is coming from a genuine place. People can tell if you put real effort and thought into your content or if you just spent a few minutes in scrubbing the internet for a top ten list of ideas. Attaching personal experience into the mix will resonate with people.

Combining these content strategies as part of your overall marketing mix will put you ahead of your competition. Having unique and creative content will implant a lasting impression in the minds of potential consumers. Content that converts potential consumers into a repeat cult following of loyal clients for your business means your content is king.

Yes, we're
OPEN
eye candy
857

– CHAPTER 20 –

Growing Your Network

Source: Every business needs a support network it can turn to for advice, to help grow its market presence, and provide referrals. Every step in growing your small business network will require you to invest in relationships with potential clients, vendors, employees, and community advocates. So, where do you start?

It is critical to your business's growth and health that you establish a network of support around you. Every small business needs to have a legion of community advocacy on its side when the business environment becomes hostile. Some of your flow of client referrals may come from other business owners you have developed a relationship with over time, who do not offer the same services as your business.

In the event your business experiences a disruption, who are the fellow colleagues in the business community that you can turn to in order to keep your business on track? It's vital to establish and maintain positive relationships within the industry or business community, for two things will come out of it: resources and opportunities.

A business grows and thrives on building relationships with people. It is very important to join or be part of a business or community network. Joining either a trade organization or a local chamber of commerce will allow your business to outreach towards experienced mentors, who have "been there and done that" in the business world. This provides you the luxury of learning from their mistakes and successes.

Joining a business or trade organization will lend your business instant credibility. Most consumers view the lone wolf as a predator out to take their money. However, when a business joins an organization, it usually must qualify under a vetting process that deems the business and its owner credible. You can make personal connections with people, some who may offer client referrals, and in turn, you may have clients you cannot serve, and will need to send them elsewhere.

Having a network will increase your purchasing power. You can get better group rates if multiple business owners join together in using a shared services model to source things like health care or office supplies. Many business organizations or trade groups have preferred vendors, which they refer to for business liability insurance, financing, or other business-to-business services; these vendors cater their expertise to a specific industry or geographic area.

When building any business relationship, the goal should be to create a mutual, or greater value, exchange. Whether it is the exchange of ideas, or client referrals or vendor referrals, keep in mind, time is money, and to waste a person's time without an equal or greater value exchange is to also waste their money, as well as your own. Business relationships should be viewed as long term. Just because you met someone today or had a discussion with a new business contact today, does not mean they are obligated to you in any way, unless of course you and the other party sign a contract. You must approach each relationship with pure intention that what you offer will uplift or enhance their life or business in one shape or form.

So, where do you go to join? There are local business organizations and trade groups which are a good place to start. Research your local Chamber of Commerce. This is the place where business owners, politics and community all come together. The Chamber of Commerce offers several opportunities to network with other businesses, which is also your audience if your business sells to other businesses.

The Chamber of Commerce is an educational resource for your business, as they will be able to connect you to information on how to acclimate your business within the local community. Also, the Chamber offers opportunities to connect with the community though a myriad of local events open to the public that give businesses an opportunity to showcase their products or services to the general local public.

Organizations, such as the National Small Business Association, National Federation of Independent Businesses, and National Business Association, are small business trade organizations that blend solving industry issues with community advocacy, to leadership in government. These organizations allow for businesses to network with each other, while providing a voice for small businesses collectively concerning regulatory matters and legislation that will either help or hurt the small business owner.

So how do you build a relationship with the community around you? Community outreach should be a priority when mapping your marketing and advertising campaign and budget. Not all community outreach costs money. Sometimes it involves investing your time. Rotary Club, Kiwanis, Elks Lodge, and the VFW-American Legion are staples in the community. They are organizations led by local business owners and community leaders that perform good works aimed at uplifting the community. Through your service in one of these organizations, you will get to develop relationships with other people who will recognize your dedication to help others. And it is by way of this, they will potentially become patrons of your business.

You can join or volunteer for other non-profit causes and groups, or just help out at local Main Street events held throughout the year. The community around you will recognize the efforts you are making to reach into your pocket and calendar to help causes that are important to them. Most local consumers will support businesses which value the things important to the consumer. You can also attend local community benefits and fundraisers. I encourage you to attend the local firehouse beefsteak dinner fundraiser. You never know who you might sit next to; they just might become your biggest client yet.

A popular way to reach local community members is through events and activities that benefit the community youth. You may choose to help sponsor a local children's youth soccer team or baseball team, or to help sponsor the high school drama club's latest production. Another idea could be to donate a prize for the elementary schools Parent Teacher Organization latest fundraiser. These are all opportunities to leave your business's calling card.

You can take the lead on reaching out to the community while furthering your establishment as a local expert. Your business could plan to host a free educational seminar on a subject matter your clients might feel is important to them. For example, if you are operating a small senior health care facility, you may want to host a free seminar on how to navigate the Medicare-Medicaid system for your loved one in need of assistance. If you own a garden nursery, you can host a free seminar on how to care for and maintain sensitive decorative plants. If you're a local construction contractor, you might be able to offer up a free seminar on how to better maintain your home and home repair hacks for the weekend warrior. You can usually reserve a meeting space at the local library if you are not comfortable hosting a seminar at your office or place of business.

Some businesses take the lead by organizing a community activity. 5K runs are a very popular way to get people to gather together for a good cause. The money raised can be donated to charity, and you have plenty of opportunities to get your business name in front of people, leading up to, during, and after the event. As the host and main sponsor, your business name and contact information would be placed on all the event's marketing materials, sign up forms, social media, and mentioned during the event. You can have a team staffing a booth or table of information made available to racers and supporters.

Some business owners volunteer their time to mentor business students. This is a great way to get to establish relationships with potentially new employees and their parents, as well as aid in the development of future business leaders, passing down knowledge from one generation to the next. If business is not your strong suit, but maybe science is, then you could lend your services to the school as a judge in their annual student science fair. You can volunteer to speak at the school's career day, when the school invites members of the business community to share with students different types of experiences they can expect in a specific job or industry setting. You may offer an apprenticeship program for students that need to earn work credits toward graduation or a course requirement.

Local farmer's markets can also be a good resource for meeting the local community. If you have a product or service that can be offered through the local farmer's market, then you are making direct connections with potential consumers. Some farmer's markets will allow you to set up a table and hand out information about your business, even if you have nothing that day to sell.

There are many activities that can bring the community together. One would be to host a car show. Car shows bring out all the toys - new and old and people will gravitate or, at the very least, slow down to see what cars are in the parking lot. Make sure your business has posted signage to let people know your business was the one that made the event possible. This is where the use of small lawn signs comes in handy. You can also host a benefit concert at the municipal park. Local cover bands will usually play for free if it is a benefit for charity, and you can ask for donations upon entry.

Another role your business can play in growing its network is becoming a member of a community activist group. This can be tricky because some community activism is driven by political agendas, and so it is important to not push an agenda or get involved with any group that requires you to vacate your personal values or alienates your clients. If you're a business that caters to female clientele like a beauty parlor, you may choose to help a community activist group that supports women who are victims of domestic violence. If your business is in the environmental industry, you may want to take up cause with a group that advocates for better environmental practices.

Whereever you choose to build relationships, make sure that you are joining because in your heart you want to make a difference, want to help others and effectively uplift the community around you. If you volunteer or join a business organization or trade group with the intent that it's all about what you can get out of someone else, your actions, words and mannerisms will speak out for your wrong intentions and people will take notice. Building a community and network goes hand in hand with lending your time, expertise, and sometimes financial resources in serving others. Remember you get back what you put out.

Section V:
Completing the Cycle

eye candy
Yes, we're
OPEN

– CHAPTER 21 –
Learning from Adversity

Source: Good small business owners are recognized for their ability to manage a profitable business; however, great small business leaders are born from adversity and because of it, become the most successful of entrepreneurs. Adversity provides the average small business owner the chance to see what their business and character is made of, and if handled appropriately, adversity will help your small business grow.

Not all business owners handle adversity the same. Some business owners have closed their doors because what was deemed a crisis at the time by the business owner, was too much risk to bear. Some business owners have an innate natural ability to shrug off just about any business catastrophe, pull themselves up by their own boot strap, and begin marching again. So, what can adversity teach us? How can adversity work to our advantage? As a small business owner, will you allow for adversity to challenge you or will you conquer it?

Before we can review external factors and challenges to our business, we must first look inward. Some adversity is of our own doing. It is impossible to be right all of the time, however, when we fail in business or make a bad business decision, we must own it. It's your mistake, and it's time to tackle it. How do you tackle your mistakes? You learn from them.

There is an old saying, "If you repeat the same mistake, it means you did not learn the lesson the first time, and it only becomes a harder lesson next time". This means that if you do not stop to take a moment to review the adversity presenting itself, reflect on the mistake you made, and change the direction of your decision-making process, the outcome will only continue to get worse. Unfortunately, as the small business owner, the buck and the responsibility begins and ends with you. So, take a moment to learn from your mistakes, and you will lower your risk of self-generated adversity.

Adversity builds character. Out of the ashes of adversity, you will develop an iron stomach for negative commentary. Whenever your business experiences something positive, it may be months or even years before your accomplishment is recognized. This is due to society's love affair and addiction with failure. For some strange reason, when someone fails, society wants to celebrate it. The King of NASCAR, Race Car Legend Richard Petty said it best,

"No one wants to quit when 'he' is losing, and no one wants to quit when 'he' is winning."

During your bout with adversity, every critic will be at your door with unsolicited opinions about what you did wrong to cause your business to fail. Adversity provides opportunity for you and your business to prove them wrong. Adversity will test the character of those around you. Do you have true friends and colleagues that support you, or are they fair weather friends? Everyone says they are there for you, and they want to be there when things are "okay"; however, when things get hard, people change their minds. Adversity will provide you the answers you seek when testing those surrounding you.

Adversity is the ultimate test of time. Will you have what it takes to wait out the challenge and fend off adversity? Will your personal ability to be patient grow, or will you become frustrated when things don't work out exactly to your demands? Adversity will help you improve your patience through your small business. You are going to need a lot of patience, because in business you are dealing with people. Not all people will understand you, especially new vendors, employees or clients that come to the table with their own expectations. Patience will become your best friend.

Adversity will help develop your judgment in making better business decisions. Guided by the lessons learned from mistakes, you will have a better understanding of timing (patience); your ability to see the signs of what is next in a business cycle and head disaster off at the pass. This comes with experience. Business owners who never have had to face a crisis never get a chance to develop better judgement.

judgement. After experiencing adversity, your senses and awareness will sharpen and heighten, and you will be more perceptive to signs of trouble before it happens, enabling you to successfully mitigate risk and keep your business on the desired track.

Your business has flaws and weaknesses - no business is perfect. Adversity will show you those flaws, allowing you to take action in making improvements where needed. This will require you to be specific and disciplined in your focus on what matters most.

After successfully navigating through several adverse challenges, you will improve at handling a crisis and managing problems. Adversity will allow you to manage future crises; you will find yourself hitting the panic button less frequently. Eventually, as a great small business owner, you will be able to manage the problem, instead of the problem managing you. Leadership during adverse situations reflect your ability to identify the source of the challenge, envision a viable solution to the problem, and implement the solution in such a way that, to everyone else, it seems like an everyday part of doing business.

Adversity will challenge the strength of your staff. Will your staff and management search for a solution or will they buckle under pressure and retreat? The way an employee or business partner perceives and accepts the challenge of adversity will provide you, the business owner, a measuring stick for the character of your staff during a difficult time.

How well your staff accepts a challenge, and their willingness to work through a problem, speaks volumes about their commitment to your business.

Not all employees will go out on a limb for the business. You will find most employees prioritize job security. If at any time an employee senses their employment at risk, most will begin to search for another opportunity. If you have employees on your staff that understand and appreciate adversity as part of the small business environment and accept that challenge, then you have an exceptional staff.

Surviving adversity sends a powerful message to your clients, staff, and competition. When your business can still deliver to its clients, regardless of the business disruption, it tells your clients that they matter most. Most people where aware that business disruption happens; however, always communicate the status of the challenge, what you're doing to tackle the challenge, and the results of your plan. Your clients will know that you are willing, against all odds, to overcome issues in meeting their expectations; this sends the message that your business has the skill of resiliency.

Resiliency is the one skill set and trait your competitors will come to envy as you begin to champion over every challenge that comes your way. Nothing can stop you when you perceive adversity as an opportunity. No other business owner will ever wish you the worst, because you "eat problems for breakfast", making your business a bigger, better competitor.

So how do you overcome challenge?

Oftentimes, many small business owners are too close to the day-to-day activity of the business, making it difficult to visualize solutions for dealing with the challenge before them.

There are numerous books and articles written on how to handle adversity. Personally, I feel many of these articles are basically intended to help the reader feel good about themselves and their problem. I have not found one that aims at providing a step by step process in dealing with a critical business crisis, the type of business crisis where everything is on the line, and I mean everything: your investment, your time, your reputation - everything.

What I provide you next comes from direct experience. I have dealt with several crisis moments as a career entrepreneur, both at my own company, and as business consultant, helping other small business owner clients work through their own situations. I have found that the following practices have served best in handling a crisis or adverse situation. This is a process, and you must pace yourself so you can explore all available options in solving the challenge. These steps are generalized so they can be applied to multiple situations.

When I am informed of a crisis or challenge, the first thing I do is take a moment to breathe. So many times, small business owners react to a crisis based on a series of things:

a negative newspaper headline or bad press piece about their business followed by phone calls from family, friends, clients, vendors, staff, or even business partners, that demand to know what's going on. Issues can arise when people arrive at the door, demanding to speak with management as they react to the emotional fear stemming from the crisis.

As a small business owner, you are captain of the ship. Remember to take a breath, a deep breath, and don't react, or make any decision on the spur of the moment. People will be shouting, demanding, and pressuring you to make decisions before you even know all the facts. You must become the voice of reason; be the steady rock during the turbulence – the captain who can navigate through the storm. But first, you must simply breathe.

Next, I silence all the noise and static and remove myself from the fury and fire. This enables me to approach the matter with a clear head. I try not to allow the panic of others to wash over me; this would only hurt my ability to see the situation with clarity. I can then proceed in taking the challenge head-on without the opinions of others, that in many cases, are not based on all of the facts.

When you learn about the challenge, it's important to know the situation and work through the emotional shock yourself. I have felt numerous emotions simultaneously when facing the challenge ahead. Emotions of anger, frustration, anxiety, fear and doubt are a normal human reactions however, you must of gain control over your emotions. Much like a general on the battlefront, you must put the emotion aside and take command of the situation.

Once I am informed of the different vantage points of the challenge, I inform my closest circles that I am aware of the situation and I am in the process of gathering all the facts. With my company, Extreme Energy Solutions, I have a Board of Directors. As a small business owner, your support system may be comprised of a manager, your spouse, your accountant, your attorney, and close mentors and advisors. It is important to demonstrate to them that you are aware of the situation and are willing to deal with the matter head on.

Before I make any decision, I collect all pertinent information. I take out a sheet of paper and write down the facts. This is when I become the investigative reporter, gathering, reviewing and separating facts from opinions. I make two columns: facts that support our ability to overcome the issue, and facts that do not favor the business. I further dig for the source of the issue. Sometimes the motive of where the challenge originated will provide great insight on the actual truth, the supporting facts, and what is just rumor. Knowing the source of the issue and the facts will place you in a position to develop a plan of action.

Next, I put together a battle plan based on a few scenarios. Just as with life, rarely do things go according to plan. I prepare a few options that I could be comfortable with, depending on any change in circumstances. I play these options out in my mind like, "if I do this, how will this work out?" and "if I make this choice, how will it affect other parts of the business?"

I also research what other business leaders have done in similar situations. I compare the severity of their business crisis to mine. I compare the choices they made, as well as the results. If the results were positive, and in the direction of the business's vision, then I enhance my action plans based on proven results.

Once I have a set of battle plans drawn up, it is time to propose them to my team. When consulting my team, all facts are presented. The source of the issue is revealed and options on how to overcome the challenge are proposed. Then it is time to sit back and listen; your team may have a different perspective based on their experience.

Their vantage point and wisdom will help you to remove poor choices and options, scaling down the battle plan to be as effective as possible. New ideas may also be proposed so be flexible in changing the plan if the ideas are more relevant to the situation. As a collective, ask the question, "Is this attainable?". Once you have a general consensus on the answer to that question, you can refine the plan or implement what you have.

Once a plan has been decided on, invest the time to implement it. Set up meetings with staff and managers, and assign tasks. It is important to also assign yourself some tasks to handle, for your role in taking action is the example of true leadership that others will follow. If you are passing the plan to others without taking any role in it, you will send the message that you are just trying to shift the responsibilities down the line, which others will resent; they may feel like the scapegoat if the plan fails.

While explaining the plan to overcome the challenge, you must transfer a sense of confidence so others will also have faith in the plan. If you have no faith in the plan or its potential outcome, then others will be hesitant to take action. Those that do, will be acting from a place of obligation, not because of their personal connection to you nor because of a belief that the plan will provide a positive result. You will want to provide supporting facts to your plan.

With the action plan underway, I usually go back and check the stats and data to monitor if the plan is working. A plan to overcome adversity is a work in progress, and new ideas can grow in the moment.

You can refine or tweak your plan based on the data of the results in real time. When results begin to reveal themselves, you must give credit where credit is due. Thank your staff and support team for their contributions, allowing for them to celebrate in the successes of overcoming the challenge. This positive energy will spur a series of small victories which will allow you and your team to be more comfortable in handling future challenges.

Once the challenge has been conquered, review with your team the practices that were most effective. This will allow for an empowered team ready for the next challenge. It is very important that you and your team reflect on what they have learned from the adverse experience, and how they felt after overcoming the challenge. If the feelings and emotions are positive, these feelings will be the feelings your team will want to remember when dealing with future challenges. As a business owner, you will want to reward your team for doing a great job.

While handling the challenge, I always have the bigger picture in mind. Knowing your why, and having a love affair and obsession with your vision, will help you see past the adversity. Some of your energy is always being directed toward your vision, your chief aim, your goals. Challenges are short- term interruptions you and your business will experience in its long-term business plan. You must see adversity as an opportunity to strengthen your business, your character, and your market presence.

eye candy
857
Yes, we're
OPEN

– CHAPTER 22 –
Planning Your Legacy

Source: How are you planning for your future? What will become of your business in ten, fifteen, or even twenty years from now, once your business has become a success, with an established clientele, staff, and vendor supplier chain? What do you want to do with your business when you are ready to retire? What is the legacy you desire to leave behind?

Every small business has a life cycle, and that life cycle is usually based on the source of the business and the business owner themselves. As much as you put thought into the beginning of your business, you must also think about the end game. Most small business owners do not think about five or ten years down the road, let alone, think about retirement or what to do with their business when they are looking to retire.

When a new business owner asks me to help them with their business plan, I always take the approach of encouraging the business owner to share their vision; then, to express what that vision would look like ten, twenty, or even thirty years from now. When the business plan is being constructed, it is built with the end vision in mind, and with steps of growth and instituted practices that assure the business owner a higher probability of having something of greater value when they are ready to exit the business.

Many small business owners overlook the importance of planning their legacy. When the time comes, after years of effort and dedication, most small business owners retire, having little or no nest egg; they find themselves wrapping up their career working for someone else.

I am not a financial advisor or planner; however, you will want to consult with one so they can help you manage the profits from your business. Setting aside a portion of your earnings for later use is part of the end game for yourself. Tithing, which many people follow, is the rule of thumb that a person sets aside ten percent of their earnings for doing God's work; you should also set aside at least another ten percent for your own retirement. Doing this as early as the business is profitable will allow you to build a retirement fund for the day when you call an end to your career. You must also discipline yourself not to dip into this fund when your business falls on hard times.

What happens with your business when the time comes to exit the business? Most small business owners review all the same options. They may be counting on a family member to continue the business, either a son, daughter, or grandchild. Some business owners may opt to leave their business to their employees, transitioning the small family owned business into an employee owned company. Some business owners will just wind down the business, selling off the remaining inventory and equipment a little at a time until it's been depleted. There is another option: selling the business.

There are things to consider when contemplating the sale of your business. Selling a business can be a very complicated process, especially if the business was in existence for a long time, and/or owns a tremendous amount of assets.

Be patient with the discovery process as it can take up to twelve months; appreciate that the process of discovery is to your benefit. It is important to become familiar with all the moving parts of selling a business ahead of time. A small business owner, who is looking to sell their venture, should have a deep understanding of the valuation process.

A properly prepared Value Proposition Memorandum is the presentation in which your business will be viewed by others. This document should be well thoughtout, comprehensive, and tell the story of the business and its operations. An introductory white paper, or sell sheet, is critical in explaining your "elevator pitch" of why this deal is such a great value to prospective ownership.

You must protect the deal, honoring the importance of confidentiality. Consider the facts of the deal, not the listing price. Business owners who aim to conclude a deal based on price, sell themselves short by ignoring other value factors. Business owners looking to exit their business should also understand that the discovery period is the pathway to the sale; they should find comfort in knowing that performing their due diligence result in a buyer, whose willing to put their money on the line to protect their future potential deal. This is a good sign that there is a serious buyer interested in your business.

You must keep in mind not to personalize the sale of your business. The "you" must not matter much. If your business can operate without the owner, it means your business has grown into a money-making machine, meaning you can command a better negotiation position. The new owner will decide who to keep aboard the ship. Your ability to give the new owner the allowance to "trim fat" from the payroll will allow more room for negotiation in other areas of calculating your exit. Unfortunately, most small business owners develop a loyalty to many employees who stuck around during the hard times; however, those employees might not have necessarily created value by way of performance.

If you're the potential buyer of a business, you also should be aware of all the factors that translate into dollars and cents, written out on the check you plan to issue to the former owner.

When exercising your discovery demands, include other hosts of fact finding practices aside from the traditional accounting. This is where, as the purchaser, you can "pick the brain" of the current business owner.

Arrange for an interview during which you can ask questions of the current owner on record. This will be important for several reasons. You will be able to obtain information to which you can refer if you find out later that the business owner misrepresented the opportunity. You will also have an opportunity to "get inside the head" of the original visionary of the business; you can have a better perspective of the business direction they were trying to achieve.

Some questions you may want to ask could include, "What are the current hazards of the business?"

This can provide insight on how to overcome challenges ahead of time. Some situations that seem like challenges to some people, may seem to be a crisis to others, and simple issues to solve by others. Ask the owner in hindsight, if they would do anything different and why. This can save you some time in re-engineering their business model. You will want to review the financials of the business; ask how these numbers attribute to the asking price of the business.

You will want to examine how the business has documented its practices and procedures. Ask the current owner how they arrived at the institution of their current business policies. You will want the current owner to disclose any liabilities, including debts, lawsuits, and/or pending regulatory matters.

Ask the current owner about what they have in store for the business in the event the business does not sell. Will they continue it? Or will they shut its doors? Have the current business owner explain what they perceive as their most valuable business relationship. This will reveal where the owner focused their time on clients, vendors, and other professionals.

During your due diligence period, it would be wise to focus discovery on specific areas that fall short of traditional accounting treatments. By reviewing the business's position on tax treatment, tax liabilities, and other debts, it will allow you to decide if you desire to proceed with the purchase. If there are accounts receivables or payables, you will want to negotiate which party will be responsible for these transactions: buyer or seller.

You will also want to determine if there are any pre-purchased services, such as insurance or advertising. Additional value or losses will accumulate depending on the status of those accounts. Demand to be relieved of any former liabilities or poor decisions made by the former management. If you are serious about the purchase of the business, you may choose to request to sit in on a day in the life of the business. This gives you first-hand knowledge on how the business operates, how customers are treated, how orders are fulfilled, and to see the employees in action.

After reviewing the discovery, conducting an owner interview, and observing the business in motion, you may opt to purchase the assets and contracts of the business, instead of the entire business entity, thus distancing you from the liabilities you did not create.

As a small business owner, you must realize the intensity of the discovery period. This understanding will allow your business to prepare a proper valuation that translates the message of the value you have created through your business. There are three basic business valuation methods in which your business can be measured: asset based business valuation, income based business valuation, or market based business valuation.

An asset-based business valuation method explores the value of a business by the total sum of money required to recreate the business equal to the current business operation. Aside from the traditional accounting within the asset-based business valuation method, items such as client list, location, intellectual property, brand creation, and other assets not allotted in accounting systems are included. Asset-based business valuation also investigates liabilities, debts, and legal actions.

The income-based business valuation method addresses the business's value under the assumptions of the income production of the business and the risk it takes to produce the income. Two factors that aid in determining how the income-based business valuation method works are capitalization and discounting. Here, the actual business risk is accounted for via the cost of return on investment of cash flow.

Market-based business valuations use a comparison method to find a business's value. Your business is compared to other businesses previously sold that contain the same or similar business product/service offerings. Usually a formal appraisal of the business, its operations, books, inventory, and assets will set the benchmarks for the value of the business. The appraisal will provide a rule of thumb when evaluating your current business against others in the same industry, and will help with setting a price that is consistent with current market values.

For a small business, there are a few methods of determining the price of your business based on metrics associated with EBITDA. EBITDA stands for *Earnings Before Interest, Taxes, Depreciation, and Amortization.* EBITDA has become one of the most important measuring instruments when valuing, pricing, selling and buying a business. However, some appraisers, CPAs-accountants, investors, and/or merger and acquisition specialists argue that EBITDA is misleading or inaccurate since the metric will exclude factors that may curb a business's real value and liabilities sometimes.

If you are thinking about buying or selling a small business, consider these rules of thumb for valuing the small business:

- 35 percent annual revenue, add fixtures, equipment and inventory;
- 2 times Yearly Seller's Discretionary Earnings (SDE) plus inventory; 4 times monthly sales plus inventory;
- 2.5 times Yearly Earnings Before Interest and Tax (EBIT);
- Earnings before Interest, Tax, Depreciation and Amortization (EBITDA).

EBITDA assists in determining how much profit a business currently makes under the present conditions of assets, operations, the products/services offered, and cash flow. The formula for calculating EBITDA is as follows: EBITDA = Revenue – Expenses (excluding taxes, interest, depreciation and amortization).

Not all business owners decide to sell their business. They can continue the business under the current management and employees by transitioning the business into an employee owned company. They can also consider converting the business into a cooperative, owned by members, who are also the clients, assuring the business lives beyond the current ownership. Co-op memberships can also be passed down from generation-to-generation of consumer.

There is the old saying, "You can't take it with you". So, what will you do with all that money? Most successful business owners understand the importance of giving back, and either contribute to a non-profit cause, or establish a non-profit entity of their own, intended on helping a cause which they value. Setting up a non-profit or foundation, is a great way to leave a long-lasting legacy of using the blessing of wealth to help others and perform God's work.

Beyond the money, and knowing that your business will continue to serve the next generation of consumer, what is the legacy you desire to leave behind? I share with my consultant clients to think about the words they wish to leave on their tombstone. Whenever asked about the final words that would be inscribed in stone, the replies were never "owner of ten fancy cars lies here". What would you want people to remember about the impact your business had on their lives?

If you could leave behind a few words of wisdom, a paragraph of advice for the next generation of up- and-coming business owners or entrepreneurs, what would you tell them? Would you tell them to make sure you cross your "t's" and dot your "i's"? Would you tell them to pay attention to the fine print? Would you tell them to stick to their core values and remember the things that helped them obtain their success in the first place?

Would you tell them about how you overcame the challenges and crises that almost ended it all? Would you tell them how many times you had no idea how you were going to cover your week's payroll during times when business was slow? Will you tell them how they must not give up on their dream, and focus their nerve beyond the worry, and on the prize? Just remember the wise words someone once shared with you that helped you launch your business, and share those words with the next crop of small business owners and up and coming entrepreneurs.

It is highly suggested that you consult and engage with the proper professionals when either purchasing or selling a new or existing business opportunity. You will want to consult and engage a certified public accountant, third party auditor, attorney that specializes in business affairs, and other experts that can vet the value of your business and investigate on your behalf as the potential buyer. Nothing in this chapter should be deemed as legal or financial advice.

eye candy
Yes, we're
OPEN

APPENDIX:

Cited Resources

(in order of appearance and usage)

1. "Small Business GDP: Update 2002-2010," published by Economic Consulting Services LLC UC Berkley, for SBA Office of Advocacy, released January 2012. Written by Kathryn Kobe

2. "What Matters More: Business Exit Rates or Business Survival Rates," published by SBA Office of Advocacy, released 2009. Written by Brian Headd, Alfred Nucci, and Richard Boden

3. "Small Business Facts & Data; Small Business Facts," published by Small Business and Entrepreneurship Council, released 2017, written by SBE Counsel Staff, www.sbecouncil.org/about-us/facts-and-data/

4. ***"Small Business at a Glance,"*** published by the International Data Group, released on 2005, written by IDC staff, www.entreprenuer.com/page216022

5. ***"Report: Small-Business Survival Rates are on the Rise,"*** published by Inc. Magazine, May 3, 2017. Written by Leigh Buchanan, www.inc.com/leigh-buchanan/kauffman-foundation-main-street-index

6. ***"10 Things to Consider When Choosing a Location for Your Business,"*** published by Entrepreneur Magazine, May 20, 2015. Written by Staff, www.entrepreneur.com/article/244866

7. ***"Choosing a Location for Your Business,"*** published by The Balance, February 2, 2017. Written by Scott Allen, www.thebalance.com/ choosing-a-location-for-your-business-1201032

8. ***"The Best and Worse States to Start a Business,"*** published by Business Insider, October 22, 2016. Written by Andrew Depietro, www.businessinsider.com/the-best-and-worse-states-to-start-a-business-2016-10/#-2

9. ***"The Best and Worst States for Business 2016,"*** published by Forbes, November 16, 2016. Written by Kurt Badenhausen, www.forbes.com/sites/kurtbadenhausen/2016/11/16/the-best-and-worst-states-for-business-2016/#39bbb2621477

10. "The 5 Best States to Start Your Small Business," published by The Hartford Small Biz Ahead, March 29, 2017. Written by Alexander Huls, www.sba.thehartford.com/ business-management/the-5-best-to-start-your-small-business

11. "Where to Get Money to Start a Business," published by Business Know How, April 3, 2017. Written by Janet Attard, www.businessknowhow.com/money/startup-money

12. "Where to Find Startup Business Loans 2017," published by Nerd Wallet, March 7, 2017. Written by Benjamin Pimentel, www.nerdwallet.com/blog/small-business/start-up-business-loans-for-bad-credit

13. "The Truth about Small Business Grants from the US Government," published by Thought Co., May 4, 2016. Written by Robert Longley, www.thoughtco.com/small-business-grants-from-the-government-3321957

14. "Creative Finance, Here's Where to Find the Money in a Credit Crunch," published by Startups, June 2009. Written by Tom Nawrocki, www.entrepreneur.com/article/202102

15. "Small-Business Grants and Resources for Veterans 2017," published by Nerd Wallet, January

1, 2017. Written by Steve Nicastro, www.nerdwallet.com/blog/small-business/small-business-grants-for-veterans/

16. "Starting a Business without Funding," published by Biz Connect, April 2017. Written by Biz Connect Staff, www.bizconnect.standardbank.co.za/start/funding/reference-documents/starting-a-business-without-funding.aspx

17. "Beyond the Bank Loan: 6 Alternative Financing Methods for Startups," published by Business News Daily, September 29, 2016. Written by Jennifer Post, www.businessnewsdaily.com/1733-small-business-financing-options-

18. "Accelerators vs. Incubators: What Startups Need to Know," published by Tech Republic, November 17, 2014. Written by Connor Forrest, www.techrepublic.com/ article/accelerators-vs-incubators-what-startups-need-to-know/

19. "11 Places to Find Money to Start a Business," published by Forbes Magazine, April 10, 2014. Written by Kerry Hannon, www.forbes.com/sites / nextavenue/2014/04/11-places-to-find-money-to-start-a-business/#658a2a59151d

20. "5 Best Ways for Funding a Startup," published by Inc. Magazine, 2017. Written by Adam Heitzman, www.inc.com/adam-heitzman/5-best-ways-for-funding-a-startup

21. "4 Realistic Ways to Fund Your Small Business," published by Forbes, August 29, 2013. Written by Brent Gleeson, www.forbes.com/sites/brentgleeson/2013/08/29/4-realistic-ways-to-fund-your-small-business/#6338361740be

22. "The Benefits of EDI," published by GSX, a GSX White Paper, January 2011. Written by GSX Staff, all rights reserved

23. "Types of Inventory Control Systems," published by Paragon U, May 11, 2015. Written by Jerad Dowler, www.paragon-u.com/types-of-inventory-control-systems

24. "The Complete List of Time Management Tools for Small Businesses," published by Hub Works, 2016. Written by Hub Works staff, www.hubworks.com/blog/time-management-tools/

25. "Best Payroll Services for 2017," published by Business News Daily, March 17, 2017. Written by Chad Brooks, www.businessnewsdaily.com/7509-best-payroll-services.html

26. "5 Time Management Tools for Small Businesses to Improve Productivity," published by Entrepreneur Magazine, Feb. 1, 2016. Written by Dipti Parmar www.extrepreneur.com/article/254812

27. "5 Social Media Management Tools to Save Time," published by Social Media Examiner, April 18, 2016. Written by Ken Waldman

28. "8 Ways to Keep Your Employees Happy," published by Mashable.com, December 4, 2013. Written by Lauren Drell

29. "Hiring Your First Employee," published by Entrepreneur Magazine, 2017. Written by Erika Welz, www.entreprenuer.com/article/83774

30. "10 Hiring Tips for Your Small Business," published by Masable.com, December 28, 2013. Written by Lauren Drell

31. "Seven Tips for More Effective Small Business Hiring," published by Forbes, July 25, 2014. Written by Andrew Schrage,

32. "Admitting Your Weaknesses and Hiring to Support Them," published by Fast Company.com, April, 2, 2014. Written by Steven Sinofsky, www.fastcompany.com/ 3028473/admitting-your-weaknesses-and-hiring-to-support-them

33. "Branding the Right Message About Your Business," published by www.Sam Burlum.com, October 31, 2016. Written by Samuel K. Burlum

34. "Essential Must Have Marketing Tools for Small Business," published by www.SamBurlum.com, December 30, 2016. Written by Samuel K.

Burlum

35. "3 Ways Online Reviews Benefit Your Business," published by Manta.com, April 3, 2017. Written by Brook Preston, www.manta.com/ resources/ publications/tip-of-the-day/

36. "Top 10 Free Online Marketing Tools for Small Business Owners," published by Code Condo.com, January 16, 2014. Written by Alex, www.codecondo.com/free-marketing-tools-small-business/

37. "Why Content Marketing is King," published by Entrepreneur Magazine, October 20, 2011. Written by Mikal E. Belicove, www.extrepreneur.com/article/220587

38. "Why Blog? The Benefits of Blogging for Business and Marketing," published by Hub Spot, September 30, 2015. Written by Corey Wainwright,

39. "The Nine Ingredients that Make Great Content," published by Kissmetrics.com, 2017. Written by Zach Bulygo, www.blog. kissmetrics.com/ingredients-of-great-content/

40. "6 Keys to Writing Effective Blog Post," published by Imagine Business Development, April 25, 2017. Written by Doug Davidoff, www.blog.imaginellc.com /the-importance-of-blogging-6-keys-to-writing-effective-blog-posts

41. *"Blogging is More Important Today Than Ever Before,"* published by Social Media Today, April 6, 2013. Written by Nicole Beachum

42. *"Trade Associations Can Help Boost Your Business,"* published by Transfirst.com, February 14, 2013. Written by Beth Longware Duff

43. *"3 Business Valuation Methods,"* published by The Balance, December 16, 2016. Written by Susan Ward, www.thebalance.com/business-valuation-methods-2948478

44. *"5 Common Business Valuation Methods,"* published by SecureDocs.com, January 22, 2014. Written by Larua Fanundes, www.securedocs.com/blog/2014/01/the-5-most-common-business-valuation-methods

45. *"6 Factors in Taking Over an Existing Business,"* published by Entrepreneur Magazine, October 26, 2015. Written by Jared Hecht, www.entrepreneur.com/article/249944

46. *"10 Questions You Must Ask Before Buying a Business,"* published by Entrepreneur Magazine, December 19, 2012. Written by Jane Porter. www.entrepreneur.com/article/225090

47. *"10 Things to Do Before Selling Your Business,"* published by Seattle Business Magazine, 2017.

Written by Dan Wright

48. "10 Things to Look Out for When Buying a Business," published by Entrepreneur Magazine, November 23, 2005. Written by Cliff Ennico, www.entreprenuer.com/article/81176

49. "What is EBITDA," published by Business News Daily, February 25, 2015. Written by Katherine Arline. www.businessnewsdaily.com/ 4461-ebitda-formula-definition.html

50. "How to Build a Legacy Brand in Your Small Business," published by Succeed as Your Own Boss.com, May 2, 2017. Written by Melinda Emerson, www.succeedasyourownboss.com/build-legacy-brand-small-business/

51. "The 5 Things Entrepreneurs Must Know When Selling a Business," published by Forbes, September 3, 2013. Written by Holly Magister

52. "What You Need to Know Before Selling Your Business," published by Inc. Magazine, 2017. Written by John Burley, www.inc.com/john-burley

53. "Second Nature Selling," published by Ecoceptor LLC, 2010; Written by Michael C. Holler and Samuel K. Burlum, a coursework and Seminar Manual

eye candy
Yes, we're
OPEN

APPENDIX:
GLOSSARY

Accredited investor - A person or entity that can deal with securities not registered with financial authorities by satisfying one of the requirements regarding income, net worth, asset size, governance status or professional experience.

Advertising - The activity or profession of producing information for promoting the sale of commercial products or services.

Angel investor - Usually, a former entrepreneur or professional who provides starting or growth capital in promising ventures, and helps with advice and contacts. Unlike venture capitalists, angel investors usually operate alone (or in very small groups) and play only an indirect role as advisors in the operation of the investee firm. They are deemed to be "angels in comparison with grasping investors who are termed "vulture capitalists".

Assets - Something valuable that an entity owns, benefits from, or has use of, in generating income.

Barriers to entry – Economic, procedural, regulatory, or technological factors that obstruct or restrict entry of new firms into an industry or market. Such barriers may take the form of (1) clear product differentiation, necessitating heavy advertising expenditure to introduce new products, (2) economies of scale, necessitating heavy investment in large plants to achieve competitive pricing, (3) restricted access to distribution channels, (4) collusion on pricing and other restrictive trade practices (such as full-line forcing) by the producers or suppliers, (5) well established brands, or (6) fierce competition.

Barter - Trading in which goods or services are exchanged without the use of cash. Resorted to usually in times of high inflation or tight money, barter is now a common form of trading in deals such as offers to buy surplus goods in exchange for advertising space or time.

Benchmarks- Performance goals against which a business's success is measured. Benchmarks help determine whether a business is on target of its expected growth compared to other like kinds of businesses.

Bootstrapping - A type of business funding that seeks to avoid relying on outside investors. Boot strappers usually rely on personal income and savings, sweat equity, lowest possible operating costs, fast inventory turnaround, and a cash-only approach to selling.

Branding - The process involved in creating a unique name and image for a product in the consumers' mind, mainly through advertising campaigns with a consistent theme. Branding aims to establish a significant and differentiated presence in the market that attracts and retains loyal customers.

Business accelerator – Accelerators are organizations that offer a range of support services and funding opportunities for startups. They tend to work by enrolling startups in months-long programs that offer mentorship, office space and supply chain resources. These business accelerator programs offer access to capital and investment in return for startup equity.

Business development - Business development relates to the process of identifying and executing agreements with potential new customers, with a focus largely on new business, new opportunities and new ways of partnering with others to deliver to new customers. It also refers to partnering with other companies to deliver product to customers or securing preferential supplier arrangements. Business development is that first point of contact and relationships, after which customers are handed off to other aspects of the marketing and selling team in terms of responsibility.

Business incubator - An incubator is essentially an organization that provides startups with a shared operation space. Incubators also provide young businesses with networking opportunities, mentoring resources and access to shared equipment. Business incubators do not generally put a time stamp on their support programs.

Capitalization (4) - 1. Accounting: Recording of a cost as a fixed asset (written off as depreciation over several accounting periods) instead of an expense (charged off against earnings in one accounting period). 2. Corporate: Conversion of the retained earnings of a firm into capital through a new issue of stock. 3. Finance: Structure and amount of long-term equity and debt capitals of a firm expressed as percentage of the total (equity and debt) capital. 4. Leasing: Conversion of an operating lease into a capital lease by classifying the leased asset as a purchased asset, and showing the lease obligations as loan on the books of the lessee firm.

Cap rate - The discount rate used to determine the present value of a stream of future earnings. Typically this will be an appropriate risk-free return plus a premium to reflect the risk of that specific investment.

Cash flow - The discount rate used to determine the present value of a stream of future earnings. Typically, this will be an appropriate risk-free return plus a premium to reflect the risk of that specific investment.

Cost of goods sold – This is an alternative term for *cost of sales*. In manufacturing, it is the sum of direct material, direct labor, and factory overheads incurred in making a product. In retail, it is the purchase price of merchandise.

Crowd funding - The method of raising money from a large number of individual investors, typically through the Internet, for a project or organization.

Cryptocurrency - A purely digital form of money. The first cryptocurrency that began trading online was Bitcoin in 2009. The main difference between cryptocurrency and physical currency is that only a fixed amount of cryptocurrency is produced by the entire system as a whole. No one person or the government has the authority to create more cryptocurrency and the rate at which it is produced is bounded by a set value and the information is publicly available. There are many different cryptocurrencies, with Bitcoin still being the most widely recognized.

Due diligence- The careful and though process in which a party in a business transaction is allowed to examine discovery, perform inquiries, conduct interviews, and research a business opportunity before they decide to move ahead with the business transaction.

EBITA - *Earnings Before Interest, Taxes, Depreciation and Amortization.* An approximate measure of a company's operating cash flow based on data from the company's income statement, calculated by looking at earnings before the deduction of interest expenses, taxes, depreciation, and amortization.

Economy of scale - Reduction in cost per unit resulting from increased production, realized through operational efficiencies. Economies of scale can be accomplished because as production increases, the cost of producing each additional unit falls.

Entrepreneurship - The assumption of risk and responsibility in designing and implementing a business strategy or starting a business.

Equity – The Vaue of a property minus liens or claims; Ownership interest in a corporation in the form of common stock or preferred stock; total assets minus total liabilities.

Exit strategy - The way in which an investor plans to close out an investment/business owner. For example, a venture capitalist or angel investor/ business enterprise may look to an IPO or acquisition as his/her exit strategy; also called liquidity event.

Factoring (purchase order financing) - The selling of a company's accounts receivable, at a discount, to a factor, who then assumes the credit risk of the account debtors and receives cash as the debtors settle their accounts. Also called accounts receivable financing.

Franchise - A form of business organization in which a firm which already has a successful product or service (the franchisor), enters into a continuing contractual relationship with other businesses (franchisees), operating under the franchisor's trade name and usually with the franchisor's guidance, in exchange for a fee.

Free enterprise (system) - Business governed by the laws of supply and demand, not restrained by government interference, regulation or subsidy; also called free market.

Innovation – The creation of new product or services.

Institutional financing – Financing provided by an institution, as opposed to retail investors.

Legacy planning - A more holistic approach to estate planning. It is the creation of a definitive plan for managing your total wealth while you're alive, distributing your estate how you choose after your death, and a clear plan to pass on your legacy. Your estate includes all assets of any value that you own.

Liability - An obligation that legally binds an individual or company to settle a debt. When one is liable for a debt, they are responsible for paying the debt or settling a wrongful act they may have committed.

Limited Liability Company (LLC) - A type of company, authorized only in certain states, whose owners and managers receive the limited liability and (usually) tax benefits of an S Corporation without having to conform to the S corporation restrictions. An LLC is an unincorporated association, is relatively flexible and simple to set up (making it appealing for small businesses with only one owner), and allows for pass-through income taxation.

Market disruptor - A disruptive innovation is an innovation that creates a new market and value network, and eventually disrupts an existing market and value network, displacing established market leading firms, products and alliances.

Marketing - The process by which products and services are introduced to the marketplace.

Merchandising - The activity of promoting the sale of goods at retail. Merchandising activities may include display techniques, free samples, on-the-spot demonstration, pricing, shelf talkers, special offers, and other point-of-sale methods. According to American Marketing Association, merchandising encompasses "planning involved in marketing the right merchandise or service at the right place, at the right time, in the right quantities, and at the right price."

Net operating income - Amount by which operating revenue exceeds operating expenses in an accounting period, without taking into account the extraordinary gains and losses as well as financial expenses (such as income taxes or interest paid) and financial revenue (such as interest earned).

Operating agreement - A legal document for the purpose of giving a detailed connection between a company and one or more of its investors in setting up and operating a program to make investments.

Retailer - A business or person that sells goods to the consumer, as opposed to a wholesaler or supplier, who normally sells their goods to another business.

Risk - 1. A probability or threat of damage, injury, liability, loss, or any other negative occurrence that is caused by external or internal vulnerabilities, and that may be avoided through preemptive action. In finance, the probability that an actual return on an investment will be lower than the expected return. Financial risk is divided into the following categories: Basic risk, Capital risk, Country risk, Default risk, Delivery risk, Economic risk, Exchange rate risk, Interest rate risk, Liquidity risk, Operations risk, Payment system risk, Political risk, Refinancing risk, Reinvestment risk, Settlement risk, Sovereign risk, and Underwriting risk.

Small business enterprise - Sometimes called a small business, a small-scale enterprise is a business that employs a small number of workers and does not have a high volume of sales. Such enterprises are generally privately owned and operated sole proprietorships, corporations or partnerships.

Sole proprietorship - The simplest business form under which one can operate a business. The sole proprietorship is not a legal entity. It simply refers to a person who owns the business and is personally responsible for its debts.

Start-up- is a new small business venture or new entrepreneurial venture which has not yet made a market entry.

Supply chain - Entire network of entities, directly or indirectly interlinked and interdependent in serving the same consumer or customer. It is comprised of vendors that supply raw material, producers who convert the material into products, warehouses that store, distribution centers that deliver to the retailers, and retailers who bring the product to the ultimate user. Supply chains underlie value-chains because, without them, no producer has the ability to give customers what they want, when and where they want, at the price they want.

Sustainability - 1. General: (1) Ability to corroborate or substantiate a statement. (2) Ability to maintain or support an activity or process over the long term. 2. Economics: Continued development or growth, without significant deterioration of the environment and depletion of natural resources on which human well-being depends. This definition measures income as flow of goods and services that an economy can generate indefinitely without reducing its natural productive capacity.

Tax credit - Prepaid income tax (such as that deducted from dividend payment) that can be offset against the total income tax payable by an entity.

Valuation - 1. General: Appraising or estimating the worth of something having economic or monetary value. 2. Insurance: Determination of the worth of the asset to be insured or that which has been damaged or lost. 3. International trade: Determination of the dutiable value of imports by the customs authorities. The GATT (now WTO) Customs Valuation Code obligates the signatory governments to use the transaction value (actual price paid by the importer to the exporter) as the principal basis for imposing duties. Where transaction value cannot be used, the secondary basis of value, such as transaction value of identical or similar merchandise, computed value, or deductive value may be used. 4. Securities: Placing a value on a stock based on the market value of the issuer's assets and the outlook for its earnings.

VC group (Venture capital) - Startup or growth equity capital or loan capital provided by private investors (the venture capitalists) or specialized financial institutions (development finance houses or venture capital firms). Also called risk capital. Venture capital is a type of funding for a new or growing business. It usually comes from venture capital firms that specialize in building high risk financial portfolios. With venture capital, the venture capital firm gives funding to the startup company in exchange for equity in the startup. This is most commonly found in high growth technology industries like biotech and software. A person who deals in venture capital is a venture capitalist, and usually works for a venture capital firm.

APPENDIX:
Additional Small Business Resources

Association of Washington Business: Since its' formation in 1904, Washington's oldest and largest business association continues to serve as the states' chamber of commerce, as well as the manufacturing and technology association. AWB advocates on behalf of businesses of all sizes and from all industries, working to unify and find solutions to issues facing Washington employers, their employees and communities. AWB is located at: 1414 Cherry St. SE, Olympia, WA 98501, toll free number: 800-521-9325, e-mail: members@awb.org. Additional information can be found on their website: https://www.awb.org

Badger Barter: Badger Barter is the mid-west's largest and most active business to business bartering platform, with thousands of local and regional businesses and companies engaged in membership. Badger Barter is connected to worldwide bartering groups, which are connected to corporations that utilize Barter, allowing for you to designate your barter credits for other products-services outside the mid-west. Badger Barter is located at: 1500 W. Main Street, Sun Prairie, WI 53590; phone: 608-837-0525; or visit Badger Barter at www.BadgerBarter.com

Count Me In for Women's Economic Independence: Founded in 1999, Count Me In for Women's Economic Independence is a non-profit organization that provides financial assistance, business coaching and consulting services to woman-owned businesses. CMI relies on three basic programs with which to accomplish their mission: an online community for women business owners, and two awards – the "Make Mine a Million $ Business" and the "Micro to Millions" awards. CMI can be reached through email at: @ CountMeInforWomensEconomicIndependence. Additional information can be found at: http://www.countmein.org.

Entrepreneurs' Organization: Founded in 1987, EO is a global business network that enables business owners to learn from each other by providing numerous resources to assist in educating and inspiring personal and professional growth. EO has international locations in Singapore, Belgium, Panama, and Canada, EO's global headquarters is located at: 500 Montgomery Street, Suite 700, Alexandria, VA 22314, telephone: 1-703-519-6700. Additional information can be found on their website: https://www.eonetwork.org.

FundingPost: For over 16 years FundingPost has endeavored to globally connect entrepreneurs with leading investors through their use of various mediums, such as Venture Capital Events, Webinars, Books and their online Venture Exchange. FP is located at Second Venture Corporation, 7365 Main Street, Suite 324, Stratford, CT 06614, telephone: 860-261-2322. Additional information can be found on their website: http://www.fundingpost.com.

Minority Business Development Agency: Minority Business Development Agency is an agency of the US Dept. of Commerce. Their focus is to assist in the development and growth of minority-owned businesses, utilizing private and public sector programs, policy, and research. Additional information can be found at: https://www.mbda.gov.

National Association for the Self-Employed: Since 1981, NASE – the National Association for the Self-Employed, has been the nation's leading resource for entrepreneurs, utilizing publications, media relations and a foundation with which entrepreneurs and their small businesses can benefit from. It is the largest nonprofit, nonpartisan association of its kind in the US. NASE is located in Annapolis Junction, MD 20701-0241, telephone: (US) 1-800-649-6273 and (AK & HI) 1-800-232-6273. Additional information can be found on their website: http://www.nase.org.

National Business Association: The National Business Association (NBA) has been working alongside small business owners for 35 years, providing resources and benefits needed for business owners to succeed. The NBA can be reached by telephone: 1-800-456-0440. Additional information can be found on their website: nationalbusiness.org.

National Federation of Independent Businesses: Founded in 1943, the National Federation of Independent Business (NFIB), is the largest small business association in the US, working to defend the right of small business owners to own and operate their businesses without undue government interference. NFIB has offices in all 50 state capitals, including Washington, D.C., with its headquarters in Nashville, Tennessee. They can be reached by calling: 1-800-NFIB-NOW, or 615-872-5800. Additional information can be found on their website: www.nfib.com

National Minority Supplier Development Council: National Minority Development Council is a non-profit organization that advances business opportunities for certified minority business enterprises and connects them to corporate members, building long term strategic partnerships which encourage economic commerce between large corporate interests and locally developed small businesses owned by minority men and women. NMSDC also assist minority owned small businesses to obtain their certifications. NMSDC is located at 1359 Broadway, 10th Floor, Suite 1000, NY, NY 10018. You can also call NMSDC at (212)-944-2430 or through the NMSDC website: www.nmsdc.org

National Retail Federation: The National Retail Federation (NRF) is the world's largest retail trade association, representing retailers from over 45 countries, including the US. Their mission is to use advocacy, communications and education with which to promote the best interests of the retail industry. The NRF is located at 1101 New York Ave. NW, Washington, DC, telephone: 1-800-673-4692, or 1-202-783-7971. Additional information can be found on their website: https://nrf.com.

National Small Business Association: Since 1990, the National Small Business Association, Inc. has provided small business owners, their employees, and retirees access to innovative services, resources, and benefits, such as collegiate scholarship awards to eligible NSBA members and their families. The NSBA is committed to small business advocacy and public awareness. Located in Carefree, Arizona 85377, telephone: 1-888-800-3416, and email: contact@nsba.net. Additional information can be found on their website: http://www.nsba.net.

Owner Operators Independent Drivers Association: Starting in 1973, the international Owner-Operator Independent Drivers Association represents the interests of independent owner-operators and professional drivers on every issue affecting truckers in all 50 states and Canada. OOIDA seek to ensure that truckers are treated with equality and to ensure highway safety and responsibility among all highway users, as well as improve the business climate for all truck operators. Located at 1NW OOIDA Drive, Grain Valley, MO 64029; telephone: 1-800-444-5791. Additional information can be found on their website: http://www.ooida.com.

Small Business Administration: Founded on July 30, 1953, the US Small Business Administration focuses on four main venues with which it works: assistance to capital, entrepreneurial development, government contracting and advocacy for small business across the United States. The SBA provides millions of loans, loan guarantees, contracts, counseling sessions and various other forms of resource and assistance to small businesses. The SBA has several key locations, with a toll-free number: 1-800-827-5722. Additional information can be found on their website: https://www.sba.gov.

Small Business Association of America: Since 1964, The Small Business Association of America has provided insured benefits, discount benefit plans and services to its members, who included small business owners, those self-employed, individuals and families. Monthly dues are required. SBA is a non-profit organization located in Washington DC. Additional info can be found on their website: https://www.sbaamerica.com

Small Business International: Small Business International provides guidance and resources when a small business entertains the possibility of connecting with international partners, including matching products and services with over 80,000 other members. Business can find out more information about importing or exporting, trade laws and compliance, and more. Visit Small Business International at www.smallbusinessinternational.com

Small Business Owners & Professional Association: Small Business Owners and Professionals Association of Canada is a non-profit organization founded with the mission to provide small business owners, their employees and retirees access to a wide variety of services, programs, information and benefits, such as sponsorship activities, networking opportunities, scholarships, and advocacy, all to aid in the success of their businesses. Additional information can be found on their website: http://sboapa.org.

United States Association Small Business & Entrepreneurship: The US Association of Small Business and Entrepreneurship is an organization that seeks to assist the entrepreneurship community through teaching, scholarship, and practice opportunities. The USASBE includes members who are teachers, researchers, program directors and practitioners. Located at: 1214 Hyland Hall, 800 W. Main St., Whitewater, WI 53190, telephone: 262-472-1449. Additional information can be found on their website: http://www.usasbe.org.

US Chamber of Commerce: Founded on April 22, 1912, The US Chamber of Commerce is the world's largest business organization representing the interests of over 3 million businesses with 3 main areas of focus: advocacy, community, and leadership. Members include mom-and-pop shops, local chambers, large corporations and leading industry associations. The USCC is located at: 1615 H Street, NJ, Washington, DC 20062-2000, telephone: 1-800-638-6582. Additional information can be found on their website: https://www.uschamber.com.

US Dept. of Commerce: The US Department of Commerce was created to promote job creation and economic growth, focusing on five key areas in business: trade and investment, innovation, data, operational excellence, and the environment. The USDC is located in all 50 states and over 86 countries worldwide. The USDC's mailing address is: US Dept. of Commerce, 1401 Constitution Ave., NW, Washington, DC 20230, telephone: 202-482-2000. Additional information can be found on their website: https://www.commerce.gov.

World Green Energy Symposium: The World Green Energy Symposium enables individuals to meet buyers and investors, as well as listen to key note speakers addressing the most current vital information surrounding the global market in the Green Energy Industry. For questions on registration email: event@wges.us, telephone: 571-403-2035. Additional information can be found on their website: http://www.wges.us.

Young Entrepreneurs Council: Young Entrepreneurs Council provides all the tools needed for its members to become successful business entrepreneurs. The YEC staff utilize their extensive knowledge, networking opportunities, media exposure, and personal branding development to bring their members from novice to polished professional. YEC is located at: 745 Atlantic Avenue, Boston, MA 02110, email: info@yec.co. Additional information can be found at: https://yec.co.

ABOUT THE AUTHOR...

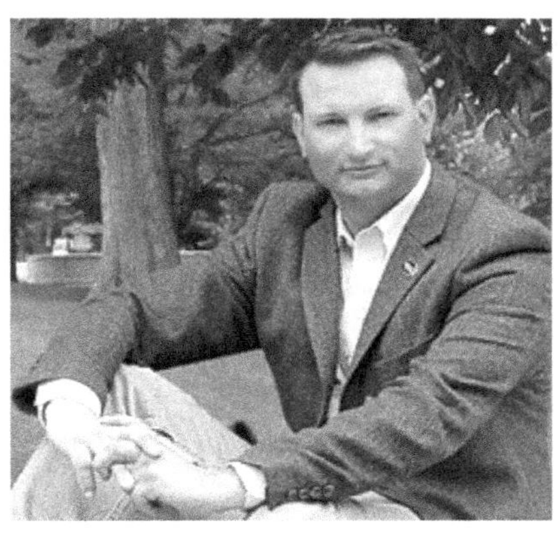

Samuel K. Burlum is a career entrepreneur, author and investigative reporter, whose career dates back to 1992, when he founded his first business. Burlum's area of expertise has been within the "green" industry, including green technology, green related consumer products, and public policy relating to environmental concerns.

Mr. Burlum holds an Associate's Degree in Applied Sciences, having majored in Business Management while attending Berkeley College, Woodland Park, New Jersey.

Currently Mr. Burlum is the CEO and President of Extreme Energy Solutions, Inc., a green tech company which brings to the market green, eco-friendly consumer products and emissions reduction technology for the automotive and transportation industry.

Burlum is a consultant for small to medium businesses, specializing in providing them guidance and expertise in the areas of strategic business planning, business development, supply chain management, and systems integration.

He is also the author of "The Green Lane," which is the compilation of syndicated articles and a column that reports on public policy debates and concerns focusing on small business and environmental justice.

His contributions to public policy include formal testimony at hearings related to air and water quality. Mr. Burlum also provided content for consideration with regards to new legislation of environmental compliance, small business research and development, technology, and tax code reform.

Burlum has been recognized by the World Green Energy Symposium, being awarded the 2013 NOVA Award on behalf of Extreme Energy Solutions for their contributions in the field of green technology, specifically addressing the issue of toxic harmful vehicle emissions while increasing engine efficiency.

He also was recognized by the People of Distinction Humanitarian Foundation and named as one of their 2014 Unsung Hero Award recipients by the foundation.

The Passaic Valley FOP 181 recognized Burlum and his company in the field of environmentally- friendly products and services, naming his business Company of the Year in 2013, 2015, and 2016, while also naming Burlum a leader in the community.

He has been featured on media venues such as *Today in America* with Terry Bradshaw and Cablevision's *Neighborhood Journal*, as well as in *Natural Awakenings* Magazine.

Books by Burlum include; "The Race to Protect Our Most Important Natural Resource, Water," Sam Burlum's Main Street Survival Guide for Small Businesses," and "Life in the Green Lane - in Pursuit of the American Dream."

Samuel Burlum currently resides in scenic Sussex County, New Jersey, not far from his home town of West Milford, New Jersey.

For more information, you can reach Mr. Burlum by visiting his website at

www.SamBurlum.com

eye candy
Yes, we're
OPEN

OTHER BOOKS BY SAMUEL K. BURLUM:

"Life in the Green Lane; in Pursuit of the American Dream"

Based on a true story…

"Life in the Green Lane; in Pursuit of the American Dream," is based on a true story, written by Samuel K. Burlum. This story explains the journey and experiences of a group of individuals that participated in one of the largest open source research projects in postmodern times, responsible for spurring off the green technology revolution in the field of fuel economy.

Led by a small group of people with a vision, they would take on the responsibility of legitimizing a movement into an industry segment within the automotive and green tech sector, sharing their challenges and trials along the way.

When it is discovered that the controversial Hydro Assist Fuel Cell can deliver beyond early expectations, in specific applications, it is met with great resistance from media, government, and industry skeptics.

"Life in the Green Lane; in Pursuit of the American Dream," is a true David versus Goliath story, in which Samuel K. Burlum tells his side of the story regarding the series of events on how one group of individuals became the trend setters in taking an obscure technology and launching it main stream.

Burlum shares the full details behind the science of fuel economy, and how he and his team deployed the Smart Emissions Reducer technology into the market. He also provides a full account of trials, challenges, and behind – the-scenes battles that he, his team, and his company had to overcome in bringing this innovation to market.

Order Online Today:

https://www.indiegogo.com/projects/life-in-the-green-lane-based-on-a-true-story-entrepreneurship#/

http://samburlum.com/about-life-in-the-green-lane/

Or you can order "Life in the Green Lane," through the mail by using the form on the next page...

ORDER FORM:

"Life in the Green Lane- in Pursuit of the American Dream"

- Written by Samuel K. Burlum

Complete the information below, and then select the items you wish to buy. Send this form & your check/money order payable to:

Sam Burlum, PO Box 730, Hewitt, NJ 07421

You should receive your order within 7 to 10 business days of us processing your payment and confirming your order. We thank you for your business in advance.

Type of Book Copy	Cost Each	No. of Copies	Total
Soft Cover	$24.99		
Hard Cover	$39.99		
E-book Version on CD	$9.99		
	Total	Order:	$

Includes FREE Shipping & Handling Cost

Name: ______________________________

Mailing Address: ______________________

City/State/Zip Code: ____________________

Phone/email: __________________________

OTHER BOOKS BY SAMUEL K. BURLUM:

"The Race to Protect Our Most Important Natural Resource-Water"

A view into our most precious natural resource; the continued public policy debates that affect our ability to preserve and protect clean fresh drinking water supplies; and how you can play your role in providing clean water to the tap;

The Race to Protect Our Most Important Natural Resource-Water is a book which explores the current geo-political climate and public policy debates surrounding water preservation and conservation, and what, as individuals and communities, you can do to aid in protecting our society's most important natural resource-water.

Samuel K. Burlum shares the perspective of how dwindled clean drinking water supplies have shaped economies and communities of the past, and where today's most threatened clean drinking water supplies are located.

This book gives a comprehensive viewof a number of available technologies aimed at cleaning up the murky waters, polluted water supplies, and how to transform dirty water supplies into useable tools that keep our society moving.

This work offers a number of solutions that individuals can put to practice in preserving and conserving clean drinking water supplies in their home, while also educating readers on methods to mitigate pollution at the tap and at the source.

Forward by Dr. Carley Corrado, PhD; *"The Race to Protect Our Most Important Natural Resource"* is "a race that we cannot lose," added Francis Okelo, Former Ambassador & United Nations Special Envoy

Order Online Today:

Amazon

Barnes & Nobles

http://samburlum.com/

Or you can also order "The Race to Protect Our Most Important Natural Resource: Water," by completing the form on the next page

ORDER FORM:

"The Race to Protect Our Most Important Natural Resource-Water"

– Written by Samuel K. Burlum

Complete the information below, and then select the items you wish to buy. Send this form & your check/money order payable to:

Sam Burlum, PO Box 730, Hewitt, NJ 07421

You should receive your order within 7 to 10 business days of us processing your payment and confirming your order. We thank you for your business in advance.

Type of Book Copy	Cost Each	No. of Copies	Total
Soft Cover	$14.95		
E-book Version on CD	$4.99		
	Total	Order:	$

Includes FREE Shipping & Handling Cost

Name: ______________________________

Mailing Address: ______________________________

City/State/Zip Code: ______________________________

Phone/email: ______________________________

ORDER FORM:

Order a Copy Today for A Friend

"Sam Burlum's Main Street Survival Guide for Small Businesses"

– Written by Samuel K. Burlum

Complete the information below, and then select the items you wish to buy. Send this form & your check/money order payable to:

Sam Burlum, PO Box 730, Hewitt, NJ 07421

You should receive your order within 7 to 10 business days of us processing your payment and confirming your order. We thank you for your business in advance.

Type of Book Copy	Cost Each	No. of Copies	Total
Soft Cover	$24.95		
Hard Cover	$34.95		
E-book Version on CD	$4.99		
	Total	Order:	$

Includes FREE Shipping & Handling Cost

Name: ______________________________

Mailing Address: ______________________________

City/State/Zip Code: ______________________________

Phone/email: ______________________________

FOR MORE INFORMATION:

For more information about the author, Samuel K. Burlum, or to subscribe to his monthly articles, sign up today at:

www.SamBurlum.com

You can also visit these other websites for more information about other eco-friendly green technology and products:

www.ExtremeEnergySolutions.net

www.SmartEmissionsReducer.com

www.ExtremeKleaner.com

www.H2OEnergyFlow.com

Or you can join Samuel K. Burlum and the affiliated products on Social Media:

eye candy
857
Yes, we're
OPEN

CPSIA information can be obtained
at www.ICGtesting.com
Printed in the USA
BVHW070721220119
538280BV00001B/71/P